Theo-
logy
&
Life

THEOLOGY AND LIFE SERIES

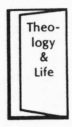

Volume 26

TRADITION AND TRANSITION
Historical Perspectives on Vatican II

by
John W. O'Malley, S.J.

Michael Glazier
Wilmington Delaware

ABOUT THE AUTHOR

John W. O'Malley, S.J., is currently Professor of Church History at Weston School of Theology in Cambridge, MA. He received his Ph. D in History from Harvard University, and his areas of specialty include the history of preaching, of church reform, and of Renaissance culture and religion. Among his publications are *Praise and Blame in Renaissance Rome* and *Giles of Viterbo on Church and Reform.*

First published in 1989 by Michael Glazier, Inc., 1935 West Fourth Street, Wilmington, Delaware 19805. ©1989 by Michael Glazier. All rights reserved.

Library of Congress Cataloging-in-Publication Data

O'Malley, John W.
   Tradition and transition: historical perspectives on Vatican II / John W. O'Malley.
    p. cm.—(Theology and life: 25)
    Bibliography: p.
    Includes Index.
    ISBN 0-89453-769-5 : $12.95
    1. Vatican Council (2nd : 1962-1965). 2. Catholic Church—Doctrines—History—20th century. 3. Catholic Church—History. 4. Catholic Church—History—1965-
    I. Title. II. Series: Theology and life series : v. 25.
    BX830 1962.045   1988
    262'.52—dc19   88-39107
                                                         CIP

Series ISBN: 0-89453-295-2

For Jack and Marilyn

TABLE OF CONTENTS

ABBREVIATIONS

AAS	*Acta Apostolicae Sedis*
Catholicism	*Catholicism in Early Modern History: A Guide to Research*, ed. John W. O'Malley (St. Louis: Center for Reformation Research, 1988)
COD	*Conciliorum oecumenicorum decreta*, ed. Giuseppe Alberigo, et al. 2nd or 3rd ed. (Bologna: Herder, Istituto per le scienze religiose, 1962, 1973)
ConOecDecr	Idem
TS	*Theological Studies*

PREFACE

This volume contains six studies related to Vatican Council II that I have published over the course of the past seventeen years. The first one appeared in 1971, while three others appeared within the past twelve months. They approach the Council from a number of different aspects, but they all do so with a historical perspective and ask the basic question of the meaning of the Council for our day. That is the justification for gathering them together in a single volume.

They are published here with only a few changes, mostly editorial. In some instances I would have liked to revise some paragraphs and sections to forestall possible misunderstanding, but such an enterprise, once initiated, promised to lead to producing a different book altogether. I also believe that, taken as a whole, these studies are self-corrective, for a viewpoint that receives an almost exclusive emphasis in one of the essays is balanced with other considerations someplace else.

The reader will encounter, given the nature of the volume, a certain repetition. I beg your indulgence. At least some of the repetition takes the form of amplification and further elucidation of ideas that are treated quite sparingly the first time they appear. I have in fact arranged these studies not according to their year of publication, but according to a scheme whereby the first three raise questions in a more general way and the last three enter into more detail. I have added a Postscript in which I attempt to review the basic issues about the Council treated in the preceding pages.

ACKNOWLEDGEMENTS

"Vatican Council II," *New Catholic Encyclopedia*, vol. XVII (Suppl. 1979), 687-90.

"Vatican II: Historical Perspectives on Its Uniqueness and Interpretation," in *Vatican II, The Unfinished Agenda: A Look to the Future*, ed. Lucien Richard, with Daniel Harrington and John W. O'Malley (Paulist Press, New York, 1987), pp. 22-32.

"Tradition and Traditions: Historical Perspectives," *The Way*, 27 (1987), 163-73.

"Reform, Historical Consciousness, and Vatican II's Aggiornamento," *Theological Studies*, 32 (1971), 573-601.

"Developments, Reforms, and Two Great Reformations: Towards A Historical Assessment of Vatican II," ibid., 44 (1983), 373-406.

"Priesthood, Ministry, and Religious Life: Some Historical and Historiographical Considerations," ibid., 49 (1988), 223-57.

1

Vatican II: The Event

Pope John XXIII's announcement, Jan. 25, 1959, less than three months after his election, that he intended to convoke an ecumenical council caught the world by surprise. There was no immediately obvious crisis requiring such an extraordinary measure and, except for those areas of the world where Christianity was suffering overt persecution, the Church gave considerable evidence of vigor and self-confidence in the decade and a half following World War II. The generic reasons John gave for convoking the Council—"affirming doctrine" and "ordering discipline"—cast little light on what he intended and on the course the Council might take. A generally pastoral purpose seemed to be what the Pope had principally in mind.

Once the Council was announced, however, certain problems and even grievances began to surface to which relatively little advertence had been given until the possibility of resolving them was offered by the Council. In Western Europe and North America, especially, there was a desire to end the religious and cultural isolation in which better-educated Catholics sometimes felt themselves confined. In Germany and Holland the experience of cooperation with Protestants during World War II resulted in a desire for more active participation by the Church in the ecumenical movement. The American political experience seemed to tally ill with official Catholic teaching on the Church-State issue and some theologians hoped for a revision of that teaching. In missionary countries there was a developing sense of the inadequacy of methods of evangelization indissolubly conjoined to Westernization. The insistence upon Latin as the language of the liturgy was symptomatic of this problem. Even aside from the special problem in missionary lands, liturgists were frustrated that the general reform of the liturgy for which they had been preparing for several decades had not received a more favorable hearing in Rome. Some members of the episcopacy, moreover, had begun to express concern that over the course of the centuries their office had gradually been deprived of many of its rightful prerogatives and that the bishops had been reduced to simple executors of decisions of the Roman Curia.

The vague purposes announced for the Council thus evoked a wide range of expectations, hopes, and fears in the three and one-half years between the Pope's announcement of his decision and Vatican Council II's beginning. From the membership of the Preparatory Commissions and the work the Commissions accomplished a conservative bias became apparent. Though Pope John remained immensely popular during this period, he permitted certain occurrences interpreted by some as reactionary and even repressive. There was discouragement or alarm among those who hoped the Council would be innovative in resolving the problems emerging and already openly discussed. Among the causes of uneasiness were the conservative statutes enacted by the Roman Synod of 1960, the publication of the apostolic constitution *Veterum sapientia* in 1962 (promoting Latin), and the peremptory measure of the Holy Office in suspending from teaching two professors of the Pontificio Istituto Biblico—M. Zerwick, SJ and S. Lyonnet, SJ. These and similar actions began to create in some circles a decided animus against the Roman Curia, generally held to be directly or indirectly responsible for them. They also fostered the emergence of an ill-defined but well-publicized and very visible division among those who were to participate in the Council between "progressives" and "conservatives."

When the Council finally opened, Oct. 11, 1962, there was no clear indication of what direction it would take and which of the two wings would dominate. However, the Council was already distinguished by a number of features unique, or at least extraordinary, in the history of such assemblies. These features would contribute to the eventual domination of the Council by the progressive wing and give the Council a character quite different from that of any which preceded it.

First of all, the 2,540 churchmen with right to vote who attended the opening session vastly exceeded the 700 or so who attended the opening session of Vatican I, and the number at Vatican I was more than triple the number present at the best attended sessions of Trent. Second, the missionary countries of Asia and Africa were considerably better represented by Western and native churchmen than was the case at Vatican I, whereas there had been none present at Trent and only three at Lateran V, 1512-17. Third, the vagueness of the purposes for which the Council was convoked encouraged an examination of all aspects of ecclesiastical life and thus gave the Council an open-ended agenda.

Fourth, the decision to admit non-Catholic "observers" to the sessions of the Council was unique, allowing the deliberations of the Council to be reviewed by scholars and churchmen who did not share basic assumptions upon which Catholic theology and discipline were based. As events would prove, this decision stimulated a more searching scrutiny of conciliar documents than would otherwise have been the case, and it was important for turning the attention of the Council to the large issue of the Church's general relationship to the contemporary world. Hans Küng's *The Council, Reform, and Reunion* (New York 1961), originally published in German (Vienna 1960), was the most influential among the many publications in the preparatory years that evoked a sense of the dramatic possibilities for change.

Fifth, the interest in the Council of the communications media was aggressive. Until the Council of Trent, the deliberations of councils were almost the private concern of those who participated in them. With the invention of printing, Trent and especially Vatican I had to contend with a more general and rapid dissemination of information and propaganda, but this dissemination was still confined to a very small percentage of the world's population. Radio and television, however, were now capable of thrusting news about the Council upon the world at large almost at the very moment any newsworthy event occurred. The actions of the Council would thus be discussed and debated in the public forum on a day-to-day basis and the members of the Council would be forced to explain and justify their actions to a public which did not always understand or have sympathy with the complex questions being raised. There is no doubt that the attempt to satisfy some of the objections and problems raised by the media affected the Council's direction and imparted confidence to those members of the Council who were more progressive in outlook.

Finally, the mentality with which many of the progressive theologians and other experts approached their task was more historical than in any previous council. This mentality was the result of the revival of historical studies in the 19th century and the consequent application of historical methods to sacred subjects, particularly to the history of doctrine, discipline, and liturgy. Theologians were thus much more aware of the profound changes that had taken place in the long history of the Church than were their counterparts in earlier councils. They were also aware that many of these changes could be adequately explained in merely human terms as expressions of a given culture and that they were therefore not necessarily irreversible. This keener sense of history thus permitted greater freedom in judgment that some practices or traditions might be simply anachronistic and should be modified or even eliminated. Moreover, it was now obvious from historical studies that many of the doctrines taught by the Church in the 20th century were unknown as such in the Church of the apostolic or patristic periods. The Immaculate Conception of Mary would be an example. Theologians could not escape facing issues like these, and John Courtney Murray, SJ, one of the *periti* at the Council, stated that "development of doctrine" was "*the* issue underlying all issues" at Vatican II. For the first time in an ecumenical council, therefore, doctrinal positions had to be formulated with as much concern for historical context and process as for their validity in terms of traditional metaphysics.

All these factors contributed to the most striking characteristic of the documents the Council produced: the great scope of their concerns. The Council wished to speak "to all men," as the Constitution on the Church in the Modern World succinctly stated (*Gaudium et spes* 2). In a word, Vatican II took greater note of the world around it than any previous council, and it assumed as one of its principal tasks colloquies or conversations with that world. The Council's pastoral concerns were thus broadened far beyond the confines of the Catholic Church to a universal horizon. The Council was fully aware, therefore, that the Church was in history and in the world, and it wanted the Church to act in accordance with that awareness.

From such an awareness of history and the world, it was an easy step to the decision to make some changes in the Church in order to put it into a more effective relationship with the contemporary situation. This awareness, indeed, was the psychological matrix capable of sustaining the idea of *aggiornamento*, which came to be the theme of the Council. The decrees of the Council by and large determined that religious practice and the expression of religious doctrine should be changed by the "new era" in order to meet the needs of the "new era," as the members of the Council perceived them. Previous councils had generally insisted on the stability of religious practice and doctrinal formulas and on the necessity of eradicating anything that would threaten that stability. *Aggiornamento* took the opposite position; in the breadth of its application and the depth of its implications, it was a revolution in the mentality with which previous councils had addressed their problems.

In the time that has elapsed since the close of the Council in December 1965, it is clear that the Council had a dramatic impact on the life of the Church. This impact is principally due to three factors, already described. (1) The decisions of the Council were communicated to the Church and to society in general with an effectiveness inconceivable without modern developments in the media of communication. (2) The open-ended agenda resulted in a series of documents which touched every aspect of ecclesiastical life, including public and private expressions of piety. (3) The historical mentality which accepted change as a normal feature of religion reversed the common persuasion among Catholics that their cult and fomulations of belief were immune to change.

The changes which resulted were in part legislated by the Council or by other authoritative documents which later implemented conciliar decrees. A series of documents emanating from the Holy See, for instance, greatly modified liturgical and sacramental practice, especially for the Eucharist and the Sacrament of Penance or Reconciliation. Religious orders revised, sometimes radically, their dress, their discipline, and even the apostolic scope of their activities.

Other changes were due to the initiatives and experimentations which the Council encouraged without being overly specific as to what forms these initiatives and experiments might take. The Council's affirmation of the ecumenical movement and its concern for justice and peace in the world resulted, for example, in more effective collaboration of Catholics and Catholic organizations with others. On a deeper level, Catholic religious instruction attempted to renew what was distinctive of Roman Catholicism by stressing, *inter alia*, those beliefs and values which Catholics shared with others. There was considerable effort in seminaries and elsewhere to base the teaching of theology more directly on the text of Scripture, and the Scholastic base on which Catholic theology had rested for centuries was decidedly challenged.

Despite the public debate on individual issues during the Council, the changes in practice and the change in mentality which the Council seemed to demand were thrust upon a Church not wholly prepared to understand or receive them. Although the progressive wing eventually came to dominate the Council and generally seemed to enjoy public approbation during the course of the Council, its viewpoints often could not be translated into action without offending the religious sensibilities even of many who felt sympathetic to the general direction the Council took. The faithful, as a body, remained conservative, and their expectations of the Church were sometimes far removed from what *aggiornamento* in its sweeping breadth seemed to require.

Thus, a period of considerable turmoil ensued in the years immediately following the Council. In some parts of the Church, there was a marked decrease in candidates for the priesthood and religious life, and, to a degree unprecedented since the Reformation, mature men and women left the priesthood and religious orders. Certain countries registered a decrease in attendance at the liturgy and a general decline in religious practice. The very viability of the so-called institutional Church was called into question by some scholars and responsible observers.

The disquiet in the Church was in part symptomatic of a more widespread disquiet throughout the world which erupted unexpectedly towards the end of the 1960's and which sometimes resorted to violence in its protest against various institutions, programs, and ideologies. Nonetheless, the unrest in the Church testified to the perception many Catholics had that a significant change had been effected in their religion as they had known it. From the viewpoint of Church history, it can be asserted that never before in the history of Catholicism had so many and such sudden changes been legislated and implemented which immediately touched the lives of the faithful, and never before had such a radical adjustment of viewpoint been required of them.

If these changes are located in the broad course of Church history, they can be assessed as attempting the following reforms. (1) There was a reversal of the process of centralization of authority in the Holy See which originated with the Gregorian Reform of the 11th and 12th centuries and which continued until the opening of Vatican II, with a moment of special strength achieved by the definition of papal infallibility at Vatican I. (2) There was a moderation of that influence of Greek metaphysics on the formulation of beliefs which had been operative since the patristic era and sanctioned by the Scholastic enterprise of the High Middle Ages. (3) There was a concomitant attempt to insert into doctrinal formulations some considerations of a more biblical and historical character. (4) A more appreciative attitude developed towards other religious communities, and especially towards the Christian Churches with origins in the crisis of the Protestant Reformation in the 16th century. (5) Catholics became more deeply engaged in problems of justice and peace in the world at large, thus complementing their engagement in more narrowly ecclesiastical enterprises. (6) A style of piety was fostered based more directly on biblical sources and on the public liturgy of the Church, to replace the so-called "devotionalism" and the paraliturgical practices that had characterized the late Middle Ages and had showed great vitality in the 19th and early 20th centuries. (7) There was a deemphasis of the distinction between clergy and laity, which had received particularly sharp formulation during the Gregorian Reform and its aftermath, and which tended in practice to reduce the role and dignity of the laity in the Church. (8) There emerged a greater sensitivity to local needs and customs, especially in missionary lands, and an effort to abandon the presupposition of European cultural superiority dominant in missionary efforts since the Chinese-Rites controversy of the 17th century.

With certain qualifications, therefore, it can be asserted that the Council dealt with a number of issues whose origins dated from the Middle Ages and the Counter Reformation and that it tried to reverse or to moderate considerably positions that crystallized at those crucial periods of Church history. No previous council had ever been so ambitious in its program.

2

Vatican II:
Historical Perspectives on
Its Uniqueness and Interpretation

More than twenty years after the close of Vatican II, Roman Catholics still find themselves being exhorted from all sides to its implementation. Widely divergent interpretations of the Council, however, especially concerning Church order, pastoral practice and the exercise of theology manifest themselves ever more insistently and find echo even on the front pages of our daily newspapers. It is difficult to implement something whose directives are disputed. Interpretation of the Council is thus at present as burning an issue as it has ever been and, to many people, an increasingly distressing one.[1] Why is this so? That is the question that, from the perspective of a Church historian, I will address in this chapter.

To contextualize the question, we must constantly remind ourselves of certain features that are special to Vatican II and that, when taken as whole, make it quite different from any council that preceded it. Obvious among such features is the sheer number of participants with the right to vote, triple the

---

[1]See Karl Rahner, "Towards a Fundamental Theological Interpretation of Vatican II," *Theological Studies*, 40 (1979) 716-27. Worth reading is the article by Andrew Greeley, "The Failures of Vatican II after Twenty Years," *America*, 146, no. 5 (Feb. 6, 1982) 86-89, and the various responses in the same journal, 146, no. 23 (June 12, 1982) 454-61.

number present at most sessions of Trent. Similarly dispro-
portionate to both Trent and Vatican I was the far greater
representation from countries outside Western Europe. It could
be argued, moreover, that the Council was the longest in the
history of the Church—not surely in the span of years over
which it extended but in terms of continuous working hours,
particularly if we should count the work of the commissions
done between the four great periods of the Council. Never
before at any council had such an elaborate and broadly repre-
sentative apparatus of theological scholarship been devised
and put into such effective operation. The decision to admit
non-Catholic "observers" was unique in the annals of such
gatherings, at least in the arrangements and spirit with which it
was carried out.[2]

Limitations of space do not allow me to elaborate on the
implications of these and similar features, but even the simple
enumeration of them substantiates a peculiar character for the
Council and suggests that problems of interpretation might
arise. There are other features, however, that are more pertinent for our purposes and upon which I would like to dwell.
Two of them can be joined together to help explain why the
Council has been unique in the way it has touched the lives of
the faithful and caused them so much concern. Those features
are the relationship of the media to the Council and the content
of many of its documents.

We take the media so much for granted that we forget what
an immense influence it has on our lives and that it therefore
perforce had on the Council and its aftermath. At least until
the Council of Trent, the deliberations and decisions of
councils were almost the private concern of those who participated in them. With the invention of printing, Trent and
especially Vatican I had to contend with a more rapid diffusion
of information and propaganda, but this dissemination was
still confined to an extremely small percentage of the world's

---

[2]The admission of Lutherans at the second period of Trent, 1551-52, for instance,
took place in an entirely different atmosphere. See Hubert Jedin, *Geschichte des
Konzils von Trient*, 4 vols. (Frieburg, 1949-75), III, 292-314, 359-99.

population. Most Catholics probably had no idea Trent was even in session, and the implementation of its decrees had its effect only over the course of many decades, even centuries.[3] Radio and television were by 1962, however, capable of thrusting news about the Council upon the world at large almost at the very minute any newsworthy event occurred. In the stages preparatory to the Council, the Vatican adopted a decidedly cautious attitude toward the media, but pressure from a world accustomed to open dissemination of information was too great to be resisted.[4] "Public opinion" became a major issue, and, because of the media, participants in the Council were constrained both in Rome and at home to explain and justify the actions of the Council not only to the Catholic faithful but to the world at large. No thinking Christian concerned about the future of Christianity was deprived of information, and, indeed, such information was eagerly sought.

As it turned out, the information was not dull or without import for the daily life of every Catholic. This is another feature that makes Vatican II altogether unique in the history of ecumenical councils and helps account for the sometimes acrid debates about it. Councils in the past have with few exceptions dealt with abstruse doctrinal or disciplinary matters that had little immediate relationship to the devotion of the ordinary faithful or, at most, affected only a single territory or level of society—certainly not true of Vatican II! First in order of immediate impact were the decree on the liturgy and the subsequent series of documents emanating from the Holy See that dealt with it. Every practicing Catholic had to be aware of these changes—changes that he saw taking place with his own eyes and at the very heart of what Catholics had learned their lives should center upon, the Eucharist.

Within a few years after the close of the Council, the entire liturgy of the Church was celebrated in the vernacular. This

[3]See Giuseppe Alberigo, "The Council of Trent" in *Catholicism in Early Modern History: A Guide to Research*, ed. John W. O'Malley (St. Louis, 1988).

[4]See, e.g., Xavier Rynne, *Vatican Council II* (New York, 1968) 51-52.

was only the most obvious change, which had even deeper ramifications. In fact what happened was a complete reorientation of Catholic devotional life. A style of piety now came to be promoted that was based more directly on biblical sources and on the public liturgy of the Church, replacing the so-called devotionalism and the "paraliturgical" practices that had characterized the late Middle Ages and had shown great vitality in the nineteenth and early twentieth centuries. An extensive system of novenas, Stations of the Cross, Forty Hours, "miraculous medals," parish missions and other usages passed out of existence almost overnight and found partial replacement in Bible study groups, directed retreats, and liturgical workshops.

The decrees on ecumenism and on religious liberty had similar, though not quite so immediately striking, repercussions. In some countries the latter decree had important legal ramifications, as the idea of an official religion of the state gradually lost ground. Concomitant with these developments was the gradual lifting of episcopal prohibitions in the United States, for instance, of Catholics attending non-Catholic colleges and universities. The Index of Forbidden Books, still a subject of perturbation for some Catholics as late as the 1960's, was now seen as outmoded and was soon forgotten, just as it had for long been unenforceable.[5]

The list of changes in practice and attitude that were mandated or encouraged by the Council could be lengthened, but enough has been said to indicate why the Council was immediately perceived as so important. From the viewpoint of Church history, it can be categorically asserted that never before in the history of Catholicism had so many and such sudden changes been implemented, often without adequate explanation, that immediately touched the lives of all the faithful, and never before had such a radical adjustment of attitude been required of them.

---

[5]See, e.g., the last paragraph of the article (1967) on "Index of Forbidden Books," in *New Catholic Encylopedia*, VII, 434-35. On the origins of the Index, see Agostino Borromeo, "The Inquisition and Inquisitorial Censorship," in *Catholicism*.

The impact of the media and the very content of the documents explain, therefore, why Catholics feel such a stake in the Council, and they further indicate why the interpretation of the Council has become so problematic. Christianity is by self-definition traditional. Its obligation is to "tell the next generation" the message it has received. Any too sudden or too obvious change in practice or attitude is bound to be scrutinized for possible adulteration of that fundamental commission. Vatican II could not hope to be exempt from the law, and, given the wide variety of cultures that Catholicism embraces and the wide variety of expectations it encourages, some divergence in interpretation of the conciliar documents was inevitable.

These factors do not fully explain, however, the present situation, in which not this or that prescription of some particular document seems to be at issue but rather the whole meaning of the Council.[6] Was the Council just an "adjustment" of certain practices or attitudes, or was it a wholly new orientation that cannot be so neatly tied down? Is the Council over, in that we adhere rather literally—and somewhat selectively— to its statements, or has it only just begun, in that the very heart of the Council was its openness to future developments? Though crudely put, these seem to be some of the major issues in play today. Further considerations must be adduced, therefore, to explain adequately the breadth and the depth of the present crisis, which has been notably accentuated in the last five years or so.

The first such consideration concerns not the specific content of the documents of the Council but their general scope and their style. Among the elements that make Vatican II unique in the history of ecumenical councils is the scope of its concerns and the scope of the persons it addressed. The vague purposes for which John XXIII convoked the Council allowed and even encouraged a review of every aspect of Catholic life.[7]

---

[6]See, e.g., Alberto Abelli, "Ein Grundgesetz der Restauration? Zum Entwurf einer 'Lex fundamentalis' der Kirche," *Herder Korrespondenz*, 33 (1979) 36-43.

[7]See *Acta Apostolicae Sedis*, 54 (1962) 788.

In this regard, only the Council of Trent provides a precedent, and an imperfect one at that. Although Trent undertook a general reform of the Church, its basic impulse, especially as the years rolled on, was to purify rather than change the status quo. Trent addressed, moreover, exclusively "churchy" issues, without ever embarking on an enterprise as daring as *Gaudium et spes.*

That document is unique in the annals of conciliar history not only in that it tried to deal with a broad range of social issues, thus breaking with the time-honored practice of dealing only with dogmatic or disciplinary matters, but also in that it addressed "all persons of good will," not just Roman Catholics.[8] With such a document we have, in effect, a partial redefinition of the function of the Church in the world, a long and extremely important codicil to *Lumen gentium.* In a less dramatic mode the documents dealing with ecumenism, the Eastern churches and similar matters do the same. This is a new phenomenon, one that expresses *in actu exercito* the richness of the message of the Council but that also points to its unique nature. We really have no historical precedents that will help us deal, not so much with particulars that these documents indicate, as with the fact of their existence in this context.

The very breadth of the issues that the Council chose to review and reformulate and the all-inclusive audience that the Council finally chose to address would seem to suggest that we are facing a major turning point in the history of Catholicism, at least in intent.[9] These facts would, then, further suggest that the burden of proof rests upon those who would propose a minimal interpretation of the Council, not upon those who see it as an event with more radical implications. Otherwise the massive documentation that the Council produced stands as a theatrically ostentatious exercise in announcing that nothing of great moment has happened.

[8]See *Documents of Vatican II*, ed. Austin P. Flannery, rev. ed. (Grand Rapids, 1984) 904.

[9]See my "Developments, Reforms," 107-11 below.

What in fact did happen emerges only when we place the documents in their precise historical context and do not treat them as enunciations of eternally valid platitudes. If we follow such a methodology, a fair, but not exhaustive, list of the aims of the Council would go something like this: to end the stance of cultural isolation that the Church was now seen as having maintained; to initiate a new freedom of expression and action within the Church that certain Vatican institutions were now interpreted as having previously curtailed; to distribute more broadly the exercise of pastoral authority, especially by strengthening the role of the episcopacy and local churches vis-à-vis the Holy See; to modify in people's consciousness and in the actual functioning of the Church the predominantly clerical, institutional and hierarchical model that had prevailed; to affirm the dignity of the laity in the Church; to establish through a more conciliatory attitude, through some new theological insights and through effective mechanisms a better relationship with other religious bodies, looking ultimately to the healing of the divisions in Christianity and the fruitful "dialogue" with non-Christian religions; to change the teaching of the Church on "religious liberty" and give new support to the principle of "freedom of conscience"; to base theology and biblical studies more firmly on historical principles; to foster styles of piety along the lines I indicated above; to affirm clearly that the Church was and should be affected by the cultures in which it exists; finally, to promote a more positive appreciation of "the world" and the relationship of the Church to it, with a concomitant assumption of clearer responsibility for the fate of the world in "the new era" that the Council saw opening up before its eyes. Surprisingly enough for some of us, the present conflict over interpretation of the Council revolves around just how seriously and radically these goals are to be taken—and in certain instances, it seems, whether they were really goals at all.

Perhaps just as important as the comprehensive scope of the documents is their style. Even a cursory glance at them shows that Vatican II is notably more verbose than any council that preceded it and also less technical in its language. The traditional style of conciliar documents has been the terse form of the canon, which in a few words proscribed some belief or practice. The canons reflect by their form the presumption that a council is basically a judicial or legislative body, convoked to resolve some immediate and well-defined problem or set of problems. The language is, within certain limits, juridical and precise. The first real break in this tradition came with the Council of Trent, which decided to issue along with canons the so-called "chapters" that would present the positive teaching against which the ideas condemned in the canons erred.

In the documents of Vatican II, no canons appear. The fact is undeniable, its implications great. The Council forged almost overnight a new language for conciliar, even theological, discourse. That discourse attempted to appeal to affect, to reconcile opposing viewpoints rather than vindicate one of them, and was notably exhortatory, almost homiletical in its style. That style was calculated not so much to judge and legislate as to prepare individuals for a new mind-set with which to approach all aspects of their religious lives. The traditional function of a council thus in effect underwent a notable reformulation.

One might hesitate to apply here the axiom that the medium was the message, but I must say that I continue to be surprised at how little study has been directed to the rhetoric of the Council, when we have learned over and over again that content cannot be divorced from style or literary form. If the style is the man, can we not assume, at least for the sake of discussion, that to some extent the style is the Council—and then, by extension, that the style is the Church? If we wish to interpret the Council, we must begin to pay attention to this aspect of it, rather than focusing exclusively on the content proposed in certain documents or paragraphs. Here, if ever, proof-texting shows its well-known limitations.

This subject is so complex that not much more can be done here than call attention to it and to invite scholars from various disciplines to investigate it. The limitations of the style of discourse the Council adopted are many. I have elsewhere called attention to them and have termed that style as "soft rhetoric."[10]

The Council addressed almost every aspect of Christian attitude and affect and called for some radical revisions. Though it was marked by considerable optimism about the realization of those revisions, it also was cautious about now explicitly condemning what had been for so long normatively in place. Thus the documents have a kind of detached quality to them, suspended somehow above the historical situations that they were aimed at changing. Since enemies and abuses are not named as such, the documents have a vagueness that opens them to a variety of interpretations, especially by persons untrained in the exegesis of historical texts. Since they are committee documents, moreover, they evince a flaccid quality that, at least at the distance of over twenty years, weakens the dramatic punch many of them in fact in their substance delivered.

More important than these limitations, however, are the positive implications of the new conciliar rhetoric. Vocabulary is an important constituent of style, and we could do worse in trying to interpret the Council than to draw up a list of characteristic words—characteristic in that they occur often and in that they occur for all practical purposes for the first time in official Church documents.

Surely important among these words is "dialogue"[11] It was so characteristically attributed to the Council that it turned into jargon, and one became almost ashamed to use it. That lamentable fact should not obscure for us, however, the profound implications of the term, especially for a Church accustomed to a "from-the-top-down" style of dealing with both its members and outsiders. Dialogue is horizontal not vertical, and it implies, if it is to be taken seriously, a shift in ecclesiology more basic than any single passage or image from *Lumen*

---

[10]See ibid, 97-102, 111-15 below.

[11]See *Documents of Vatican II*, e.g., 325, 470, 744, 904, 924.

gentium. But this fact emerges only when we stop concentrating on such passages and images and then look to the new style that pervades practically everything the Council said.

Other words must be added to the list—"cooperation," "solidarity," "service," "dignity." Attention must also be given to traditional words or expressions that have disappeared, and to others that are in effect redefined, like "prophet," "king," and "priest." We hear much about the "spirit" of Vatican II, but that expression wallows in subjectivity and vagueness until rescued by studies that can ground it in the conciliar texts with a methodology along the lines I am suggesting. In other words, it is possible to retrieve some sense of the "spirit of Vatican II," but we must employ a methodology that until now has not been widely applied and is only imperfectly formulated.

The verbosity of the documents of the Council often makes them boring to read, almost impossible to teach, and further complicates their interpretation. This quality indicates, however, the growing awareness of the participants of the complexity of the issues, of the wide variety of positions possible concerning them, and of the necessity of not bringing them to a premature closure. Nothing, the Council seemed to say, should be more characteristic of Catholicism than its catholicity— that is, its ability to embrace different cultures, different spiritualities and even different theologies without losing its basic identity.

The very generality of many passages of the conciliar documents does not, therefore, manifest a weakness but a strength— the strength of a long tradition that need not be defensive and that has the time to be open to opinions that seem to contradict or seriously qualify the status quo. The documents of the Council, though not all subsequent events, seemed to indicate that the lessons of the Galileo case had finally been well learned. They seemed to indicate a Church open to the future, not closed in upon its history, not even upon so glorious a moment of it as the Council itself. Their generality does, however, open them to interpretative manipulation.

Besides the scope and style of the documents, another feature of the Council that was unique was the leitmotif of *aggiornamento* that it borrowed from Pope John XXIII. The word means, literally, updating. The basic idea underlying it was, according to the Pope, to make certain appropriate "emendations" or "adjustments" in the Church that would put it in more effective touch with the world in which we live.[12] On the surface this seems to be indeed a modest proposal, and persons favoring a "strict construction" of the Council can always point to these words. A recent study has argued, however, that at least by the time the Council opened Pope John had himself come to hope for much more.[13]

In any case, the term placed Vatican II in the tradition of those councils that dealt extensively and professedly with the reform of the Church, like Constance, Lateran V and Trent. Even in this regard, however, Vatican II evinces a unique character, for the basic impulses of Catholic reform until the Council sought their goals on more timeless, less historically aware principles. Once Vatican II decided to make changes in the Church to bring it into more effective correspondence with the times, it significantly reoriented the old principle of *ecclesia semper reformanda.*

At least since the Gregorian reform of the eleventh century, no idea has had a greater impact on the history of the Western Church than the persuasion that the Church must from time to time take itself to task. With increasing insistence in the High and Late Middle Ages, the idea began to pervade the thinking of serious Christians and resulted in any number of reform movements, most graphically illustrated perhaps by the founding of so many religious orders. Despite its immense impact on the Church, the phenomenon has been curiously neglected by theologians, as if the idea were clear and without need of analysis and study. Yet it deals with the complex and fundamental problem of how an institution that is by self-definition both traditional and radical, both incarnate and transcendent, both born into a particular culture yet missioned for all times and peoples, can manage neither to turn itself into

[12]See *Acta Apostolicae Sedis,* 54 (1962) 788.

[13]See Alberto Melloni, "Formazione, contenuto e fortuna dell'allocuzione," in *Fede Tradizione Profezia: Studi su Giovanni XXIII e sul Vaticano II* (Brescia, 1984) 187-222.

a local museum nor lose itself by assimilation into its environment. It deals with and is an historical concretization of the problem of the relationship between nature and grace, between "reason" and revelation.

Distinctive of the *aggiornamento* of Vatican II in all its aspects was a keener awareness of cultural differences and the historical conditioning of all aspects of the "human side" of the face of the Church than any previous conciliar reform.[14] This was the result of the methodologies that many of the most influential *periti* brought to the formulation of the documents of the Council, whether their specialty was liturgy, the Bible, Church history, ecumenics, Church-state relations, social problems or even systematic theology. The training of most of these men had caused them to modify or move away from the so-called classicist mentality that had traditionally marked theological disciplines. The conflict between these two mentalities underlies many of the documents of the Council and is still operative today in the debate over how to interpret them.

Despite some ambivalence in the documents, awareness of historical differentiation and of the symbiotic relationship between the Church and the cultures in which it exercises its ministries is more strikingly manifest in Vatican II than in any other council. This fact again accentuates the uniqueness of the Council. For the first time, the Church officially began to take account in an across-the-board way of the profound implications of being a "pilgrim" in this world. A pilgrim is an alien, true, but also an alien on the move.

When the documents of the Council are viewed in this light, they imply an open-endedness, a certain sense of uncompleted business. If it is true that, as the times change, the Church must change with them, the process of *aggiornamento* is ongoing. By definition it cannot be statically frozen. It implies experimentation, adaptation and a keen attentiveness to the lessons of experience as we daily receive them. Those who read the documents thus must perforce clash with those whose approach is more classicist.

---

[14]See my "Reform, Historical Consciousness," below.

The turmoil into which the Church was thrown in the aftermath of the Council cannot be divorced from the cultural upheavals that took place world-wide in the late 1960s and 1970s. The blame, if it be such, for distress in the Church and for "certain excesses" can not be laid solely at the door of the Council. Nonetheless, turmoil has racked the Church at every moment of great crisis, which has generally coincided with a crisis in culture at large. We should not be surprised, therefore, at the disquiet and anguish that accompanied a Council that so expressly dealt with reforms that immediately touched the faithful and that even otherwise were so unique.

Here too we still lack adequate categories to deal with the phenomenon. I have attempted to devise a few, but they are only faltering first steps toward a more adequate hermeneutic for interpreting the Council and for interpreting similar phenomena in the history of the Church.[15] We need, in other words, further reflection on these issues that will help us better find our way. We do not need power plays that, in the name of an "authentic" interpretation of the Council, would obstruct that reflection.

[15]"Developments, Reforms," below.

3

Tradition and Traditions

My title poses perhaps the central problem in Catholic theology and spirituality today: how do we deal with our rich past so that we remain faithful to it, yet do so in a fashion that renders it engaging and life-giving? It thus poses a perennial question in Christian history, but one that Vatican Council II forced onto our awareness more urgently and dramatically than had ever been done before. In the two decades that have elapsed since the Council, the question has become probably even more pressing, as we search for 'the authentic' interpretation of what the Council intended, or even for that *sensus plenior*—bigger meaning—that might transcend the sum of the Council's documents.

Before the Council most Roman Catholics had a deep, if unreflective, belief that they belonged to a Church that 'did not change'. With the implementation simply of the decree on the liturgy, that belief was challenged in a way that no practising Catholic could ignore. Some felt betrayed, some felt liberated. All had to face the problem. With hindsight it is easy to say that a more effective catechesis was needed to prepare the faithful to understand their religion in a more sophisticated and dynamic way; a gentler style of implementation of the Council surely might have been employed. Nonetheless, the problem is so immense, so complex, so recurrent that it is difficult to imagine any catechesis fully adequate to it, especially in the climate of the 1960's.

To address the issue properly one would have to adduce the

skills of a number of disciplines—obviously philosophy and theology, but sociology, anthropology, psychology and others as well. For any number of reasons, there can be no question of my attempting that in these few pages. I can perhaps offer, however, a few reflections about how I see the issue from the viewpoint of an historian, for it touches the most crucial question with which every historian must struggle: continuity and discontinuity, duration and change. The French Revolution, all admit, was a great turning point and marked a dramatic shift in structures and mentality, but did not France after all remain French? Historians make their living on the reality of change, and the worst message they can receive is 'No news, boss'. Yet they often must reckon with the possibility that in the history of any civilization, religion or institution the continuities run deeper than almost any change.

The problem intensifies when we begin to deal with Christianity and examine it from either a theological or historical perspective. At the core of Christianity lies the belief in a message—'the Gospel', 'the Good News'. That belief postulates that the message has a validity that transcends the ages and transcends the limitations of any culture in which it finds itself, even the culture in which it first took expression. It is meant for every man and woman who ever lived or will live, and it satisfies the deepest desires of their being.

The charge of the Church was to 'hand on' that message, not adulterate or change it. But the very transcendence of the message implies that it perforce will be variously articulated and that every articulation will but imperfectly realize it. A deep continuity is postulated, yet certain discontinuities and shifts in emphasis and perspective seem equally postulated. Since they are inevitable, these discontinuities and shifts should be neither ignored nor judged negatively. They are facets of the splendor of a message meant for all, and therefore adaptable to all—while at the same time remaining true to itself. That is simply a different way of expressing the problem of the relationship of the tradition to an almost infinite variety of traditions.

As an historian of Christian culture, it has been my privilege to spend most of my adult life contemplating this fascinating phenomenon. At some moments I am struck by how continuous it is, at others by how variegated and how characterized by great shifts and revolutions. At every moment I remain impressed by the importance of studying it. That study is rewarding for many reasons, but two stand out as especially important for the situation in which we currently find ourselves.

When I speak with my students about the study of the history of Christianity, the first benefit I emphasize is that it is a liberating enterprise.[1] That study should liberate them from the 'dead hand' of the past. It can be compared to a psychological review of one's personal history that results in a series of insights as to how I came to be what I am. I am the product of a number of contingent circumstances and decisions, over many of which I had little or no control. The very insights have, however, power to enable me to stand back and assess with new eyes my present situation. I am thus liberated, at least to some extent, from forces that I previously little recognized or understood. I find myself in a new situation of freedom, and I experience at the same time a greater sense of security amid conflicting signals that come to me in the present from every side.

So much for the analogy. When we move from personal history to the broad canvas of Christianity, two rather distinct styles of reading the process of history that has culminated in the present emerge. We thus return to the problem of continuity and discontinuity. The first style emphasizes the former, often operating on the assumption that certain developments or 'trajectories' were not only appropriate under given circumstances but preordained and now irreversible. Underlying this approach sometimes seems to be almost an organic model of the historical process, as from the acorn grew the mighty oak. A review of the process of history obviously yields a better understanding of where one stands at present, but leaves little room for significant change in the future, except in the direc-

[1] See my 'Church Historians in the Service of the Church,' *Römische Quartalschrift*, 80 (1985), pp 223-34, and the three articles by John Tracy Ellis, James Hennesey and myself in *America*, 147 (1982), pp 185-93.

tion of more and better of the same. This style of reading history heavily accounts for the shock that reforms of Vatican II dealt to many Roman Catholics.

The second style places more emphasis on the discontinuities. It would underscore that the long history of Christianity is characterized by certain shifts in theological style, ecclesiastical culture, liturgical forms, Church order, and the practice of ministry and spirituality that, while of course not entirely discontinous with one another, merit the name revolution—or at least minor revolution. Moreover, these changes do not in themselves argue to an inevitable and irreversible course in one direction but express the tradition in a fashion uniquely appropriate for the culture of the day. Implied of course is that similar shifts may be possible in the future.

Let me illustrate how these two styles of interpretation work in a specific instance in the history of Christian theology and piety. It is possible to move easily from the teaching of Saint Bernard on grace to that of Saint Thomas on the same matter, to show the differences and similarities of their ideas. This is a legitimate and just enterprise. It is equally important, however, to underscore the immense cultural shift that had taken place between the time of the monastic spirituality of Bernard in the twelfth century and the academic theology of Aquinas in the thirteenth. When the two saints spoke about grace, the tune might be the same but the music was different, as different as Gregorian Chant and Beethoven's Ninth. They spoke about the same matter, but they were engaged in two quite different enterprises and conceived of theology in almost irreconcilable ways. A fully adequate historical interpretation of them must take both elements into account.

Just as important as accounting for both those elements is being on guard against the prejudice that even the history of Christianity reads like a history of progress. Despite the battering that prejudice has taken as a result of the World Wars, it is still subtly influential even in religious circles and finds a congenial colleague in a view of history that favors continuities. Was Aquinas' theology really better than Bernard's, or was it a case of gain and loss? To become more contemporary: were the reforms of Vatican Council II a definitive culmination of historical development, now frozen in their perfection, or do they not of themselves invite us to further reflection and action in a reality that, by definition, can never achieve perfect expression and requires constant readjustment?

This is not the place to enter into the complex question of how to interpret the Council, but surely it can be asserted that its *leitmotif* was the adjustment of theology, piety and ministry to 'the needs of the times'. This was only another way of putting the issue of tradition and traditions, for the transcendence of the message is all too transcendent if it precludes entrance into the lives of those for whom it was intended.

Much has been written about the ecclesiological redefinitions proposed in *Lumen gentium*, the Council's dogmatic constitution on the Church, but a more fundamental ecclesiological statement pervades all the documents of the Council. The statement is a reiteration of the basic truth that the Church is an institution of ministry, and ministry by definition adapts itself to the condition of those to whom it ministers. An ancient truth this, but the Council shifted from the more customary emphasis on the saving power of the tradition itself to the necessity of so living and expressing it that it meet 'the needs of the times'. The principle expressed in that shift allows a more open-ended interpretation of the meaning of the Council, obviously, than does an adherence to the specific stipulations of its decrees. In my opinion, it thus justifies a reading of the history of Christianity that makes more generous allowance for the discontinuities in that history than has often been verified, especially in Catholic circles.

The result of such a reading liberates us, therefore, in a twofold sense. It tells us who we are and where we are. Just as important, it suggests to us that the future is more open than we had thought, for the past is more variegated, less homogeneous, less unidirectional than we had thought. Within certain limits, reversal of course is possible. As we bring all our powers to bear on discovering and living a more perfect expression of the gospel, we simultaneously realize that these expressions will remain manifold, for they can only be articulated by human beings who are the products of manifold cultures and individual circumstances. There can be no tradition without traditions, but the latter, no matter how sincere, appropriate and well argued, possess no absolute claims. For them to be authentic, in fact, they must reduce the tradition to contingent expressions. This brings me to my second point. If the first benefit of a study of the history of Christianity is that it liberates us by giving us a new understanding of the forces that brought us to the present moment and made us what we are, the second is complementary to it. The second is an enrichment of our imaginations. While the first liberates us, in a sense, from the past, the second liberates us from the present. It is a trip to a foreign land, during which we look back to our ordinary habitation with new eyes. In the late twentieth century we are not so much victims of 'future-shock' as of 'present-shock', for the media daily bombard us with the reality of the moment and thereby deprive us of the stimulus to examine alternatives to the way things are. The drive of the contemporary world is towards a kind of world-wide uniformity, which ranges from styles of clothing to styles of thought to styles of organization in multi-national businesses and other institutions. This is as true for religion as it is for everything else.

One of the periods of Christian history that I know best is the Counter Reformation, that is, the story of Catholicism in the sixteenth and seventeenth centuries—the Jesuits, the Council of Trent, the Spanish Inquisition and all that. The popular stereotype of this period is that it was characterized by repression, codifications, orthodoxies and rigid conformism. Anybody who knows the period recognizes that the sterotype is not without basis in fact.[2] Yet, the more the period is studied, the more its variety and vitality manifest themselves—as once again the tradition refused to be confined within the limits that some would prescribe for it. The Counter Reformation was rich in traditions, some of which it inherited almost unchanged, others that it inherited and modified, still others that it created almost from new. To that extent it is a bracing experience to

---

[2]See my 'Catholic reform' in *Reformation Europe: A Guide to Research,* ed Steven Ozment (St Louis, 1982), pp 297-319, and especially the volume under my editorship, *Catholicism in Early Modern History: A Guide to Research* (St. Louis, 1988).

immerse oneself in it and thus allow one's imagination to be enriched by the wonderful variety it manifests.

In no other area, perhaps, did the Counter Reformation evince greater creativity than in ministry—and in that correlate of good ministry, spirituality. The so-called disciplinary (or 'reform') decrees of the Council of Trent can be viewed from a number of different perspectives. Taken singly they strike one today with their juridical vocabulary and their distance from our own mentality. The underlying impulse that pervades them, however, is a reform of ministry. The ecclesiological statement that they in effect make is that the Church is an institution of pastoral care—not a startling statement, but one that perfectly corresponded to what the sixteenth century needed to hear, one that constantly has to be made, and one that was reiterated, though in quite different terms, in Vatican II.

In recent years those decrees of Trent have been criticized for obstructing precisely what they hoped to obtain. According to critics, they imposed a network of 'parochial conformity' that blocked the 'natural kinships' that made medieval Christianity such a vital religion.[3] The criticism does not lack merit, especially when the truly long-range effects of what the Council set in motion are weighed. Those effects show that any remedy for abuse can itself become an abuse as times and conditions change; the tradition constantly needs to be articulated again into new traditions. Moreover, the negative effects attributed to the Council derived perhaps more from how the Council came to be interpreted over the course of the centuries than from what the Council intended, and, in any case, generally took many centuries to be felt in a large number of areas. It can hardly be denied, however, that the Council's desire to move bishops and other ministers from 'feudatories to pastors' was urgently needed at the time.[4]

At a distance of four hundred years, nonetheless, what is

---

[3]John Bossy has particularly espoused this interpretation. See, e.g., his 'The Counter-Reformation and the People of Catholic Europe', *Past and present*, 47 (1970), pp, 51-70, and his recent *Christianity in the West 1400-1700* (Oxford, 1985).

[4]See Hubert Jedin, *Crisis and Closure of the Council of Trent* (London, 1967).

most noteworthy about both the doctrinal and the disciplinary decrees of Trent is how they seem to miss the point of what was most creative and new in Catholicism at the time. The doctrinal decrees deal largely with the sacraments, in answer to Protestant attacks on them. We could easily infer that the most and best energies in Catholicism would be devoted to sacramental ministry, but this is not quite the case. It was other ministries that burgeoned, especially different forms of ministry of the Word. Although the disciplinary decrees touch on ministry of the Word in a few crucial passages, they never treat it in much detail.[5]

Neither the doctrinal nor the disciplinary decrees have anything directly to say about spirituality, yet the revitalization of older spiritualities and the creation of new ones was one of the greatest achievements of the age. With these spiritualities came new ministries, as spiritual direction and the practice of retreats assumed a role and physiognomy they had never had before. For all practical purposes, Trent has not a word to say about schools as an instrument of ministry, but the conviction was already widespread that that instrument was needed for all classes of society. Schools had never been so conceived before the sixteenth century.[6]

Even the sacraments seem to have been undergoing somewhat of a redefinition in practice, as in some circles Penance came to be envisioned less as the tribunal Trent described and more as a locus for encouragement and direction, or even for a kind of 'personalized sermon', as an early Jesuit put it.[7] These as well as many other developments were surely not contrary to the Council, but they went beyond it and did not look to it for warrant. 'From below', one might say, new traditions were being forged. The poor communications of the era did not

---

[5]The most important passages occur in Session V, 1546, 'Super lectione et praedicatione', and in Session XXIV, canon IV, 1563, 'De reformatione', in *Conciliorum oecumenicorum decreta*, ed Giuseppe Alberigo et al., 3rd ed. (Bologna, 1973), pp 667-70, 763. See also Peter Bayley, 'Preaching', in *Catholicism*.

[6]See Paul Grendler, 'Schools, Seminaries, Catechetics', in *Catholicism*.

[7]See my 'Unterwegs in alle Länder der Welt: Die Berufung des Jesuiten nach Jerónimo Nadal', *Geist und Leben* (1986), pp 247-60, especially 258.

allow for too close supervision, so these traditions were able to come into being and make their way on a trial-and-error, success-and-failure basis. Contrary to what one might expect, therefore, a reflective but nonetheless hard-headed pragmatism marked the ministry of the Counter Reformation. Even its great codifications were the result of experimentation and extensive consultation with those 'in the field'. Abstract principles were surely operative, but they were tested against practice, so that they might be made operative in an effective way. The two great codifications by the Jesuits published in 1599 illustrate this reality. The *Directory to the Spiritual Exercises* was the fruit of forty years of discussion and experience, and the same could be said for the *Plan of studies (Ratio studiorum)* intended for Jesuit schools. Especially the former is even today, moreover, remarkable for its balance and its keen perception that the same regimen is not equally helpful to all. Both documents set new traditions into place. They thus promoted them and gave them firmer form, but of course also opened the way to rigidification, literalism and even species of fundamentalism for persons with less agile minds.

Of all the initiatives of the era, few better reveal than the so-called 'missions' to rural populations the creativity of the period and the concern to adapt ministry to the specific situations—psychological and physical—of the persons for whose sake the ministry was being performed.[8] The 'missions' were not fly-by-night excursions of mindless zealots into the countryside, but carefully organized pastoral strategies. The Jesuits, Oratorians, Capuchins and Vincentians took the lead. These missions were a first experiment in 'collaborative ministry'; the missioners worked together in groups of four to eight. They generally stayed in a locality for at least a month, with a full programme in hand. The schedule of instruction, the sermons, the catechesis and the processions were adapted

---

[8]The best, all too brief, discussion in English is still by Jean Delumeau, *Catholicism between Luther and Voltaire: A New View of the Counter-Reformation* (Philadelphia, 1977), pp 189-94.

to the rhythm of peasant life, with the first exercises offered well before sunrise. Hymns were composed in the vernacular and set to the melodies of popular songs. The missioners did not abandon the locality once they had been there, but made sure to return after a few years.

As you can see, these 'missions' were composed of some traditional elements, but nothing like them was known in the Middle Ages on an organized and systematic basis. They eventually turned their attention to urban centres as well, as this Catholic 'revivalism' established itself as an important tradition in the Church well into the twentieth century.[9] It persists in some parts of the world even today.

The little Trent had to say about devotions and pious practices tended to be cautious and was as intent upon excising and reforming as in promoting them. The sixteenth and seventeenth centuries created, however, a vast and impressive new array of them. During this period novenas of all sorts, accompanied by processions, prayers and series of sermons, became for the first time a standard feature of Roman Catholic life. Along with them developed Forty Hours and similar phenomena like the *Tre Ore* on Good Friday. The Stations of the Cross emerged with a force and clearer form than they had in the late Middle Ages, and the same was true for the rosary.

Deplorable of course is how these phenomena distracted the faithful from a more properly liturgical and more directly biblical spirituality, but we should not underestimate two of their great accomplishments. First, they met people where they were and recognized that one style should not be imposed on all—they recognized the value of a variety of traditions. Secondly, they provided in most cases ample opportunity for instruction and spiritual encouragement by means of the sermons that accompanied them, in a context that gave greater latitude to preachers than did the Eucharistic liturgy.

Contemporaneous with these and many other developments within Catholicism were similar ones in the Protestant

---

[9]See, e.g., Jay P. Dolan, *Catholic Revivalism in the United States, 1830-1900* (Notre Dame, 1977).

Churches. Although the proliferation of those Churches had some obviously negative effects, it also allowed for the formulation of other traditions of piety and church order that rightly claimed a base in the tradition and surely nourished the spiritual needs of those who espoused them. If ecumenism means anything, it means that the development of these traditions within the great tradition must be examined and utilized for further enrichment of our imaginations.

But perhaps it is time we returned to the situation today. For Catholics the Second Vatican Council strove to place the Bible and the official liturgy of the Church at the centre of people's lives. For all mainline Churches the ecumenical movement has made it possible to reduce differences and to create an atmosphere in which it is possible to learn from one another. The gains in these regards, particularly in the past twenty years, have been astounding, and we should be profoundly grateful to God for them.

At the same time a certain impoverishment has ensued. What happened with Catholicism? Although it is by no means clear that the Council intended it, its decrees meant in many parts of the world such an emphasis on the Eucharistic liturgy that practically everything else disappeared, including Vespers and sermon series. Moreover, the persuasion soon seemed to be abroad that the mere translation of the liturgy into the vernacular solved all problems and that without further elaboration it would nourish all spiritual needs. Faithful adherence to the liturgical texts is important, of course, but when separated from creativity in the non-verbal aspects of liturgy it has produced in all too many churches a routinized rite that does little to engage the effect. The rubricism lamented in the preconciliar Church seems to have gone underground momentarily only to return in vernacular guise.

More broadly, the Council is sometimes seen not as providing general guidelines and opening the Church to the 'new era', as Pope John XXIII indicated, but as confining the Spirit within what is specifically prescribed or encouraged. Is this not asking too much and expecting the Council to do what no such body can? Does it not belie the fact that in the articulation of the tradition the 'normative' and the 'more authentic' are always relative to the actual needs of those for whom the tradition is intended and for whom it must find expression in a number of traditions? The abstract ideal can deliver death as well as life.

In many parts of the world Christianity remains a vital and operative reality in people's lives, but the greatest vitality and growth lies in sects, cults and in the so-called 'electronic churches'. In the mainline Churches—Protestant and Catholic—ennui, respectability and 'normative' but dull services often hold sway. Bible-thumping, glitz, ignorance and an often nasty fundamentalism mark the alternatives. It is easy to sneer at them, but we must at least concede that they have manufactured traditions that reach large numbers of people where they are. As the Vatican recently indicated, perhaps we have something to learn from this phenomenon, as we examine the problem of tradition and traditions and the liberation they both should bring.[10] Rightly understood, creativity and imagination do not militate against tradition and traditions, but are at the very heart of them.

---

[10] 'Vatican Report on Sects, Cults and New Religious Movements', *Origins,* 16 (1986), pp 1-10. An entire number of *America* is devoted to the question, 155 (Sept. 27, 1986); see especially William D. Dinges, 'The Vatican Report on Sects, Cults and New Religious Movements', pp 145-47, 154.

4

Reform, Historical Consciousness, and Vatican II's Aggiornamento

The turbulence into which Vatican II threw the Catholic Church was due not only to the abruptness with which its reform was thrust upon us. It was due as well to the fact that in our consciousness no paradigms of reform were operative which were appropriate to the reality we began to experience.[1] Despite the incalculably great impact the idea of reform has had on the thought and practice of the Western Church, theological reflection upon it has been minimal and its history has never been fully written.[2] The practical repercussions of this situation have not been happy. An almost despairing confusion has hallmarked Catholicism since Vatican II's *aggiornamento* got under way. Religious life, for instance, seemed to explode in our faces as religious orders attempted to fulfil the Council's directive to update the authentic spirit of their founders. What the Council failed to tell religious was how that authentic spirit was to be discovered, verified, and then updated or applied to

---

[1]Even today little serious literature explicitly treats the idea of *aggiornamento*, Bernard J. F. Lonergan, S.J., makes some perceptive observations in his brief "Existenz and Aggiornamento," in *Collection: Papers by Bernard Lonergan, S.J.* (ed F. F. Crowe, S.J.: New York, 1967) pp. 240-51. See also the lecture by Christopher Butler, O.S.B., "The Aggiornamento of Vatican II," in *Vatican II: An Interfaith Appraisal* (ed. John H. Miller, C.S.C.; Notre Dame, Ind., 1966) pp. 3-13.

[2]In recent years, however, some important studies have appeared. The work of Gerhart B. Ladner deserves special mention: *The Idea of Reform: Its Impact on*

"the times." The great "Council of *Aggiornamento*" did not possess or try to formulate a system of categories which was adequate to its *aggiornamento* and which would have helped us cope with the radical problematic the Council was about to ignite.

At the time of the Council we did not think to ask from it any consistent theoretical foundation for *aggiornamento*, because most of us were not even aware of the importance of having one. In view of the lack of sufficient previous academic reflection upon reform, the request would have been futile. Moreover, the news media made us cognizant of the fact that the Council's decrees were committee documents, full of compromise and ambiguity. For good reasons the decrees often eschewed technical theological language, and they did this with a realization that this procedure entailed a loss of precision and system. The Council's pastoral concerns meant that its documents were often constructed more with the hope of appealing to the affective priorities of men and women of good will than with the intention of satisfying any need for theory, even granted that providing theory was within the Council's competence.

Christian Thought and Action in the Age of the Fathers (Cambridge, Mass., 1959); "Die mittelalterliche Reform-Idee und ihr Verhältnis zur Idee der Renaissance," *Mitteilungen des Instituts für österreichische Geschichtsforschung* 60 (1952) 31-59; "Two Gregorian Letters: On the Sources and Nature of Gregory VII's Reform Ideology," *Studi gregoriani* 5 (1956) 221-42; "Vegetation symbolism and the Concept of Renaissance," in *De artibus opuscula XL: Essays in Honor of Erwin Panofsky* 1 (ed. Millard Meiss; New York, 1961) 303-22; "Religious Renewal and Ethnic-Social Pressures as Forms of Life in Christian History," in *Theology of Renewal* 2: *Renewal of Religious Structures* (ed. L. K. Shook, C.S.B.; Montreal, 1968) 328-57; "Reformatio," in *Ecumenical Dialogue at Harvard* (eds. Samuel H. Miller and G. Ernest Wright; Cambridge, Mass., 1964) pp. 172-90. In the same Harvard *Dialogue*, see the article by Martin A. Schmidt, "Who Reforms the Church?" pp. 191-206, and the report by Giles Constable, "Seminar III: Reformatio," pp. 330-43. See also Yves M.-J. Congar, O.P., *Vraie et fausse réforme dans l'église (Paris, 1950);* Jeffrey Burton Russell, *Dissent and Reform in the Early Middle Ages* Los Angeles, 1965); Nelson H. Minnich, S.J., "Concepts of Reform Proposed at the Fifth Lateran Council," *Archivum historiae pontificiae* 7 (1969) 163-251; Robert E. McNally, S.J., "Pope Adrian VI (1522-23) and Church Reform," *ibid*, pp. 253-86. I myself have tried to explore various aspects of the problem as these were illustrated in the thought of a single individual: *Giles of Viterbo on Church and Reform: A Study in Renaissance Thought* (Leiden, 1968).

Of all the affective needs felt by Catholics at the time the Council opened in 1962, few were more urgent among Europeans and Americans than the recognition that the Catholic cultural ghetto had to be terminated and a new atttitude towards the "world" had to be assumed. The Council tried to respond to this need. Perhaps the most striking characteristic of Vatican II is the scope of its concerns. The Council wished to speak "to all men" as the Constitution on the Church in the Modern World succinctly informs us.[3] In a word, Vatican II took greater note of the world around it than any previous council, and it assumed as one of its principal tasks "colloquies" and conversation with that world.[4] Its pastoral concerns were thus broadened far beyond the confines of the Catholic Church to a universal, cosmic horizon.[5] The Council was fully aware, therefore, that the Church was *in* the world, and it wanted the Church to act in accordance with the consequences of that awareness.

The Council registered its awareness of the world in at least four ways, none of them developed by any previous council. First, the Council in general evaluated the "world" positively and with some optimism.[6] Second, this positive attitude towards the world is explained by the Council's desire to see the Church be of spiritual service to the world and even to help it to its temporal fulfilment; the Church wanted to make itself an effective presence in secular society for the upbuilding of the city of man as well as for the upbuilding of the city of God.[7] Third, the Council was aware that the Church is profoundly

---

[3]AAS 58 (1966) 1026. See also *ibid.* 54 (1962) 8, as well as Paul VI's allocution to the Council, Sept. 29, 1963, *ibid.* 55 (1963) 847, 854-58. Except where otherwise indicated, all translations are my own.

[4]See AAS 58 (1966) 1010, 1058.

[5]See AAS 54 (1962) 794; 58 (1966) 947.

[6]It speaks repeatedly, for instance, of the world's social, scientific, technological, and educational "progress": AAS 58 (1966) 728, 729-30, 837, 848, 854. 1078-79. The Council's optimism about "the world," however, is not unqualified: *ibid.* 58 (1966) 704, 843, 1017, 1022, 1032, 1036, 1054-55.

[7]See AAS 57 (1965) 38, 42, 47; 58 (1966) 729, 732, 735, 739, 842-44, 862, 1060.

affected by the cultures in which it finds itself.[8] Fourth, the Council appropriated John XXIII's judgment that human society was "on the edge of a new era"; the Council wanted the Church to prepare itself to be a vitally formative influence in the "new era."[9]

From such an awareness of the world it was an easy step to the decision to make some changes in the Church in order to put it into a more effective relationship with the world. This awareness, indeed, was the psychological matrix capable of producing the idea of *aggiornamento*. Consequently, we easily accepted the idea and felt no need to probe deeply into its implications. We failed to grasp the profound shift from previous Catholic thinking on reform which was implied by Vatican II's decision to take "accommodation to the times" as the fundamental axiom of its reform.

Given the incomplete state of studies on the idea of reform, it is precarious to generalize. Nevertheless, two distinguished historians of religious reform, Hubert Jedin and the late Delio Cantimori, have independently ventured the opinion that the perennial spirit of Catholic reform was accurately epitomized by a prior general of the Augustinian order, Giles of Viterbo (1469-1532), in his inaugural address at the Fifth Lateran Council: "Men must be changed by religion, not religion by men."[10] What Vatican II's *aggiornamento* called for was precisely the opposite. It determined that religion should be changed by men, in order to meet the needs of men. Today, some years after the close of the Council, a minimalist inter-

---

[8]See AAS 57 (1965) 17; 58 (1966) 732, 968, 973-74, 1030, 1057, 1059, 1064-65, 1079.

[9]John makes this statement in the Apostolic Constitution "Humanae salutis" convoking the Council, Dec. 25, 1961, AAS 54 (1962) 6; tr. *The Documents of Vatican II* (ed. Walter M. Abbott, S.J.; New York, 1966) p. 703 (henceforth referred to simply as *Documents*). The Decree on the Bishops quotes the Pope verbatim, AAS 58 (1966) 674. See also *ibid.*, pp. 13-14, 17, 1027, 1075, as well as 54 (1962) 789.

[10]H. Jedin, *A History of the Council of Trent* I (New York, 1957) 169; D. Cantimori, *Eretici italiani del Cinquecento* (Florence, 1939) p. 6; Mansi 32, 669: "homines per sacra immutari fas est, non sacra per homines." See also Adriano Prosperi, *Tra evangelismo e controriforma* (Rome, 1969) p. 181, and my *Giles of Viterbo*, esp. pp. 179-91.

pretation of Vatican II's "accommodation to the times" no longer seems possible, no matter what the intentions of the Council fathers were. In the breadth of its applications and in the depth of its implications, *aggiornamento* was a revolution in the history of the idea of reform.

The profound implications of *aggiornamento* cannot be understood apart from the problem of contemporary historical consciousness. As in every species of the idea of reform, the *aggiornamento* of Vatican II had to deal with the question of the relationship between the past and the present. Such a relationship is implied in the very word *aggiornamento*. At every critical juncture in the Council this relationship was alluded to, usually in the form of an assurance that no substantial change was being made in the patrimony of the past.

Vatican II consistently described *aggiornamento* in terms of adjustment or accommodation. It took its cue from John XXIII's delimitation of the Council's task in his allocution opening the first session, Oct. 11, 1962, as that of introducing "appropriate emendations" into the Church.[11] On the question of doctrine, the Pope's often quoted description of the permissibility, and even necessity, of dressing up the old truths in new words indicates the mentality which was operative.[12] The conservative intent of the Pope's words is more than suggested by the fact that they seem to allude to the Dogmatic Constitution on the Catholic Faith of Vatican I.[13] What the Council attempted to do, and what it urged others to do after it, was to "return to the sources" of Christian life.[14] The purpose of this return was to see to it that in making pastoral accommodations to the modern world, even to the extent of introducing "new forms" and "innovations" and of making generous allowance for variety, only that would be changed from the past which

---

[11]AAS 54 (1962) 788.

[12]AAS 54 (1962) 792. The Constitution on the Church in the Modern World quotes the Pope, *ibid.* 58 (1966) 1083. See n. 71 below.

[13]*Conciliorum oecumenicorum decreta* (eds. Giuseppe Alberigo *et al.*; 2nd ed.; Rome, 1962) p. 785 (henceforth cited simply as *ConOecDecr*).

[14]AAS 58 (1966) 703.

was properly subject to change.[15] But events have shown how impossible it was to contain the dynamism of *aggiornamento* within modest bounds.

This brings us to the heart of the problems of Vatican II and, indeed, of any Christian reform. How are we to know what from the past can be changed? How is the present to deal with the past, and what legitimate hold does the past have on the present? What is historical authenticity, and what bearing does it have on the present? Later in this article we hope to propose some partial answers to these questions. But before we arrive at that point, it is essential to our understanding of Vatican II and to our appreciation of the problem which modern historical consciousness has thrust upon us that we try to disclose how the Council itself thought about the past. What forms of historical thinking were operative in the Council's proposed *aggiornamento*? Perhaps a helpful first step in trying to understand these forms in Vatican II would be a review of the idea of reform as it emerges in broad outline from the documents of the twenty ecumenical councils which preceded it.

The Early Councils

In the interest of brevity we shall consider the early councils from Nicaea (325) to Constantinople IV (869-70) synoptically. The basic justification for such a grouping is that they all occurred in the context of the culture of Late Antiquity, and a gap of almost two and a half centuries separates Constantinople IV from Lateran I (1123), the first of the Western and medieval councils.

Constantinople I speaks of the need of some churches for "emendation," and Chalcedon speaks of the need for "correction" in certain provinces. The former instance seems to refer to a restoration to doctrinal health of those areas touched by

---

[15]See AAS 54 (1962) 9; 56 (1964) 97, 105-6, 110, 114; 58 (1966) 706, 713, 720, etc.

heresy;[16] the latter refers to disciplinary correction, required because of a failure to hold regular episcopal synods.[17] Even Nicaea speaks of the need to "amputate" and "cut off" certain unjustified customs which have sprung up.[18] In Constantinople IV, moreover, we have several allusions to the Church as "the Lord's field" from which scandal and weeds must be uprooted.[19]

What these councils are particularly conscious of is their continuity with previous Christian belief and practice and of their solemn obligation to preserve these unchanged. Subsequent councils, for instance, are careful to affirm their adherence to the faith of earlier ones.[20] In disciplinary matters they call for the implementation of the *antiqua lex, antiqua consuetudo,* and *canonica traditio.*[21] When Chalcedon decides to invest the city of Constantinople with an ecclesiastical primacy, it justifies its action with the argument that it is following the precedent set by the "ancient fathers" in establishing the primacy of the "great Rome."[22] In more general terms, the present follows the example of the past.[23] No more accurate and succinct summary can be found of what these councils felt they were about than the statement of Nicaea II concerning its teaching on images: "We subtract nothing; we add nothing; we simply preserve unsullied all that the Catholic Church holds."[24]

Upon what presuppositions are these decisions and affirmations based? In general, they can be said to betray certain attitudes towards the past and be best understood in the context of these attitudes. First, past doctrine is normative and

---

[16]*ConOecDecr*, p. 22.

[17]*ConOecDecr*, p. 72.

[18]*ConOecDecr*, pp. 12, 14.

[19]*ConOecDecr*, pp. 136, 140, 151. Cf. Mt 13:24-25.

[20]See *ConOecDecr*, e.g., pp. 60, 63, 84, 98, 100, 103.

[21]See *ConOecDecr*, e.g., pp. 8, 11, 28, 66, 67, 73, 153, 155.

[22]*ConOecDecr*, p. 76. See also *ibid.,* p. 28.

[23]See *ConOecDecr*, e.g., p. 84 (Constantinople II): "antiquis exemplis utentes."

[24]*ConOecDecr*, p. 110: "nihil adimimus, nihil addimus, sed omnia quae catholicae sunt ecclesiae immaculata servamus..."

irreformable. Cyril's letter to Nestorius, approved by Ephesus, speaks of it as *irreprehensibilis*,[25] and Chalcedon speaks of the *inerrabilis patrum fides*.[26] Second, the councils are keenly aware of their own doctrinal and disciplinary continuity, and even identification, with earlier Christian teaching and practice. Apart from heretics or local bad custom, there is no suggestion of discontinuity or discrepancy between past and present.[27] Novelty is expressly rejected.[28] Third, the only change recognized is a change for the worse localized in particular individuals or areas, but not found in the Church as a whole. Fourth, the remedy for this individual or local deviation is removal or excision of the sick members or bad practice. Thus we have the image of the Lord's field, from which the weeds of bad doctrine or bad custom must be uprooted while leaving the good plants to grow unhindered. Fifth, in both Constantinople I and Constantinople IV we have the suggestion that the healing of disease and the removal of weeds will restore the Church to a condition of purity which she earlier had enjoyed— *prisca sanitas* and *puritas antiqua*.[29] Sixth, the past provides us with examples of how we are to conduct ourselves in the present, as in the case of trying to determine what is appropriate ecclesiastical dress.[30]

The Medieval Councils

As we move to the medieval councils between the period of the Gregorian Reform and the Great Western Schism, viz., from Lateran I (1123) to Vienne (1311-12), it is more difficult to detect the attitudes towards the past which were operative. However, there are indications that the sense of continuity was

---

[25]*ConOecDecr*, p. 36.

[26]*ConOecDecr*, p. 59.

[27]See *ConOecDecr*, e.g., pp. 27, 38-39, 47, 55, 56, 83-84, etc.

[28]See *ConOecDecr*, p. 113.

[29]See *ConOecDecr*, pp. 22, 136.

[30]See *ConOecDecr*, p. 127. See also *ibid.*, p. 84.

strong, as in Lyons I (1245), where Pope Innocent IV identifies himself with St. Peter and his prerogatives.[31] Such an attitude tallies perfectly with what we know from elsewhere about historical thought during this period.[32] From such knowledge we are led, moreover, to interpret Constitution 14 from Lyons I as suggesting a theory of moral decline in history, *hominum succrescens malitia*.[33]

What is more significant is that the word *reformare* appears for the first time in conciliar vocabulary during this period, and beginning with Lateran IV (1215) it becomes an insistent repetition. Such development was a consequence of the Gregorian Reform movement, with the awareness it produced that an improvement of morals and a return to a more ancient legal discipline was incumbent upon the whole Church. What the Gregorian Reform suggested for the first time was that not just a few isolated individuals or localities had deviated from the norm, but that moral and legal abuses were widespread, almost universal.[34]

In these councils reform was directed against bad morals and bad custom or discipline.[35] The same metaphors of weeds and sickness are employed as in the earlier councils.[36] What is distinctive of these councils, however, is the belief that certain abuses were common to almost the whole Church. As Lyons I says in Constitution 14: "Because this particular sickness is almost general, we thought it appropriate to apply a general remedy."[37] Thus the Gregorian idea that the Church as a whole might be subject to reform emerged in conciliar documents.

---

[31] *ConOecDecr*, pp. 256, 275.

[32] See, e.g., Eva M. Sanford, "The Study of Ancient History in the Middle Ages," *Journal of the History of Ideas* 5 (1944) 21-43, and Peter Burke, *The Renaissance Sense of the Past (New York, 1969) pp. 1-20.*

[33] *ConOecDecr*, p. 264. See, e.g., Ladner, "Reformatio," pp. 182-83.

[34] See, e.g., Ladner, "Reformatio," pp. 172-73.

[35] See *ConOecDecr*, e.g., pp. 174, 190, 191, 212, 217, 218, 225, 266, 285, 290, 332.

[36] See *ConOecDecr*, e.g., pp. 187, 225, 264, 266, 319.

[37] *ConOecDecr*, p. 264: "Proinde quia morbus iste quasi communis irrepsit, dignum duximus communem adhibere medelam."

Furthermore, in Constitution 50 of Lateran IV we have the first unmistakably clear conciliar statement that a change in discipline (*statuta humana*) may be required by a change in "the times."[38] This statement is remarkable not only for its bald affirmation of the necessity of adjustment to different conditions, and therefore its suggestion of historical differentiation, but also because it provides an extremely helpful criterion for deciding when a change in discipline should be effected: when required by *urgens necessitas vel evidens utilitas*.[39] Moreover, Lateran IV makes it clear that uniformity of rite and custom is by no means required of all Western Christians, and that bishops must make suitable provision for the fact that *sub una fide* there will exist *varii ritus et mores*.[40] The authentic Christian spirit, therefore, is capable of being expressed in more than one way.

Medieval conciliar reform thought climaxed in intensity at the Councils of Constance (1414-18) and Basel (1431-37). At Constance the seemingly all-inclusive formula emerged in the call for "reform of the Church in faith and morals, in head and members."[41] This reform was only imperfectly distinct from the question of ending the Schism and, as regards doctrinal reform, even less distinct from the question of the condemnation of Wyclif and Hus. Basel also issued the call for a reform "in head and members."[42] This same idea was expressed equally clearly when Basel called for a "general" or a "complete" reformation.[43] Thus the idea of a reform of the whole

---

[38] *ConOecDecr*, p. 233: "non debet reprehensibile iudicari, si secundum varietatem temporum statuta quandoque varientur humana, praesertim cum urgens necessitas vel evidens utilitas id exposcit, quoniam ipse Deus ex his quae in veteri testamento statuerat, nonnulla mutavit in novo," See also *ibid* (Vienne) p. 319.

[39] See also canon 16 of Lateran III (1179), *ConOecDecr*, pp. 195-96.

[40] *ConOecDecr*, p. 215: "Quoniam in plerisque partibus intra eandem civitatem atque dioecesim permixti sunt populi diversarum linguarum, habentes sub una fide varios ritus et mores, districte praecipimus ut pontifices huiusmodi civitatum sive dioecesum, provideant viros idoneos..."

[41] *ConOecDecr*, p. 383: "...ecclesia sit reformata in fide et in moribus, in capite et in membris." See also *ibid.*, pp. 384, 385, 392.

[42] See *ConOecDecr*, p. 433.

[43] See *ConOecDecr*, pp. 440, 443, 445.

Church reached full expression. The process of reform was still described in terms of healing disease and uprooting weeds from the field of the Lord.[44] Even though the practice of Communion under only one species was recognized as at variance with what took place at the Last Supper and with the practice of the primitive Church, Constance justifies it with the significant statement that it was introduced "for a good reason" (*rationabiliter*) and therefore would be retained.[45] Fidelity to primitive practice is thus not a norm for reform which was absolute.

The Council of Ferarra-Florence-Rome (1438-45) was principally concerned with the reunion with the "Greeks" and with securing Eugene IV's position over the latter phase of the Council of Basel. For these reasons, as well perhaps as for their by now potentially conciliarist ring, the bold phrases "general reformation" and "reform in head and members" do not appear in the Council's documents. The high tide of medieval conciliar reform had passed. However, the reunion with the Eastern Church can reasonably be considered a reform undertaking. In such a light, the principle which the Council employed to allow each Church to retain its traditional phraseology for describing the relationship of the Father and the Son to the Holy Spirit is important: under different formulas the same truth is expressed.[46] Avery Dulles finds this statement significant in the question of doctrinal reform, and he feels it implies a "principle of dogmatic pluralism" which was later lost sight of during the Counter Reformation.[47]

Lateran V (1512-17) spoke often of the need for a reform of morals, for a general reform, and for a reform "even of the Curia"; it also published several reform bulls.[48] But there is

---

[44]See *ConOecDecr*, pp. 403, 414, 432, 449.

[45]*ConOecDecr*, p. 395.

[46]*ConOecDecr*, pp. 501-2: "...et ad eandem intelligentiam aspicientibus omnibus sub diversis vocabulis.... Et cum ex his omnibus unus idem eliciatur veritatis sensus, tandem in infrascriptam sanctam et Deo amabilem eodem sensu eademque mente unionem unanimiter concordarunt et consenserunt." See AAS 57 (1965) 103.

[47]"Dogma as an Ecumenical Problem," *Theological Studies* 29 (1968) 409-10.

nothing new in its images and terminology to suggest a difference in presuppositions from preceding councils. Perhaps the most telling observation we can make concerning the Council's documents is that the cautious reform proposals and their even more cautious implementation sit ill with its seemingly clear awareness that the "times" were particularly bad and had fallen into decline.[49]

The Council of Trent

This awareness of living in evil times appears in a significantly intensified form in the documents of the Council of Trent (1545-63). On at least three occasions the Council speaks of its age as calamitous and elsewhere in unmistakable terms alludes to its particularly trying circumstances.[50] From the context of such statements we are forced to infer that the Council fathers felt a considerable decline had occurred from a better, more tranquil past when morals were purer and truth under less severe attack.

The Council, therefore, called for reform, which along with the publication of its doctrinal decrees was to be its program for settling the disturbed ecclesiastical situation. The reform it called for, we must note, was not a reform of doctrine or even a reform of the Church, but a reform of the morals "of the clergy and Christian people."[51] In other words, it was to be a reform of morals *in* the Church.[52] This reform was to be

[48]See *ConOecDecr*, pp. 571, 574, 585, 628.

[49]See *ConOecDecr*, pp. 578, 581, 583, 590, 610-11. On the question of the widespread conviction in this period that the times were worse than they had ever been, see my "Historical Thought and the Reform Crisis of the Early Sixteenth Century," *Theological Studies* 28 (1967) 531-48.

[50]See *ConOecDecr*, pp. 669, 761, 774, as well as pp. 641, 647, 712, 730.

[51]*ConOecDecr*, p. 636: "ad reformationem cleri et populi christiani"; p. 657: "depravatosque in clero et populo christiano mores emendandos."

[52]*ConOecDecr*, p. 640: "et instaurandis in ecclesia moribus"; p. 658: "et reformandis in ecclesia moribus."

effected principally by a restoration of discipline. The idea of "restoration" (*restituere, revocare, innovare*) appears often in the Council documents, and in context it must be interpreted in the sense of revitalizing the discipline or canons of an earlier age in the hope of reproducing once again the presumably better morals of that age.[53] Even in the critical question of episcopal residence, the Council affirms in Session 6 that it is renewing the "ancient canons, which have fallen into almost total desuetude due to injury suffered from men and the times."[54]

On questions of doctrine and sacramental practice no previous council ever insisted so forcefully as Trent on the identification of the present with the apostolic age or on the unchanging nature of the intervening tradition. When Trent in effect affirmed that in the Catholic Church "the ancient, absolute, and in every respect perfect (*omni ex parte perfecta*) faith and doctrine" of the Eucharist had been retained, it was only making fully explicit for one aspect of its teaching what underlies all its doctrinal pronouncements.[55] There was no question of a reform of doctrine. Though the Council "reforms morals," it only "confirms dogmas."[56] The Canon of the Church's Mass is "pure of all error," and its sacramental rites are from apostolic times.[57] The Council is careful to reject the view that the anointing of the sick or the secret and integral sacramental confession of sins might be mere human inventions.[58] What Christ and the apostles handed on, the Church retains and has always retained unchanged.[59] Before Trent the text from John's Gospel concerning the Spirit's ongoing

[53]See *ConOecDecr*, e.g., pp. 658, 663, 665, 698, 699, 712, 726, 760.

[54]*ConOecDecr*, p. 658: "antiquos canones (qui temporum atque hominum iniuria paene in dissuetudinem abierunt)...innovare."

[55]*ConOecDecr*, p. 708: "ut vetus, absoluta atque omni ex parte perfecta de magno eucharistiae mysterio in sancta catholica ecclesia fides atque doctrina retineatur,"

[56]*ConOecDecr*, p. 640: "in confirmandis dogmatibus et in instaurandis in ecclesia moribus."

[57]*ConOecDecr*, p. 710, and see also e.g., pp. 660, 679, 688, 689, 710, 730.

[58]See *ConOecDecr*, pp 681, 683, 687.

[59]See *ConOecDecr*, e.g., pp. 640, 647, 657, 669, 711, 718.

teaching mission (14:26) was used on occasion to explain a growth or increase of understanding of truth in the Church; Trent quotes it in favor of the Church's faithful conservation of apostolic teaching.[60] Trent's insistence on the identification of its teaching with that of Christ and the apostles and its corresponding insistence that the intervening tradition was undeviating is not adventitious. Sometime during the period between the Gregorian Reform and the outbreak of the Protestant Reformation there began to develop a historical sense which recognized discontinuity with the past.[61] Hence the need was felt for a "renaissance," for a rebirth of something which once was but existed no longer. This need was felt in many areas of life and culture. Petrarch, for instance, gave classic expression to it in the area of literature, and he is thereby credited with being the first person to achieve a sense of anachronism. Thus germinated the modest beginnings of modern historical consciousness.[62]

By the time the Reformation broke out, many persons in Western Europe had enough information and a sufficiently developed sense of history to think they could recognize serious discrepancies between the belief and practice of the New Testament and what they saw in the Church of their own day. In the Reformation controversies, as is clear from the famous epistolary debate between Calvin and Sadoleto, the Protestants found it to their advantage to press these real or apparent discrepancies, while the Catholics felt compelled to defend their unbroken and authentic conservation of the apostolic past.[63] Trent may occasionally soften its language, as

---

[60] *ConOecDecr*, p. 669. See *ibid.*, p. 792, for a similar idea in Vatican I. See also my "Giles of Viterbo: A Sixteenth-Century Text on Doctrinal Development," *Traditio* 22 (1966) 445-50.

[61] See, e.g., Ladner, "Reformatio," pp. 173, 176-77.

[62] See Myron P. Gilmore, *Humanists and Jurists* (Cambridge, Mass, 1963) pp. 5-19; Jaroslav Pelikan, *Historical Theology* (New York, 1971) pp. 33-43; Donald R. Kelley, *Foundations of Modern Historical Scholarship: Language, Law, and History in the French Renaissance* (New York, 1970); and Burke, *op. cit.*

[63] See John Calvin and Jacopo Sadoleto, *A Reformation Debate* (ed. John C. Olin; New York, 1966), and William J. Bouwsma, "Three Types of Historiography in Post-Renaissance Italy," *History and Theory* 4 (1964-65) 303-14, esp. 306-9.

when referring to the origins of indulgences, the doctrine on purgatory, and the practice of venerating saints,[64] or like Constance it may defend the administration of the Eucharist under only one species despite an acknowledged discrepancy with the practice of the early Church,[56] but it never swerves from the principle that the Church teaches and has always taught the apostolic truth, the whole apostolic truth, and nothing but the apostolic truth.

What Trent attempted was a moral reform of the Christian people and a reaffirmation of the Church. Constance and Basel repeatedly spoke of a "reform of the Church," but Trent never once uses the phrase.[66] The documents of Trent imply an operative distinction between the Church and the members of the Church. Individual members were subject to heresy, and according to the documents almost the whole membership seems to have been in need of serious moral regeneration. But the Church itself was as pure in its moral teaching, disciplinary practice, and sacramental rites as it was in its dogma. Individual Christians might defect and almost the whole body of Christians might suffer moral breakdown, but the Church, in an existence somehow and somewhere independent of its members, was imperturbably stable in doctrine, discipline, and rite.

Vatican I

In Vatican I explicit mention of reform occurs only twice. The first instance is in the formal decree opening the Council, which repeats almost verbatim the formula for the opening of Trent and hence speaks of "reform of the clergy and Christian people" as a purpose of the Council.[67] The second instance is in the negative sense in the Dogmatic Constitution on the

[64]See, e.g., *ConOecDecr*, pp. 750, 772.

[65]See *ConOecDecr*, pp. 702-3.

[66]*ConOecDecr*, pp. 383, 384, 385, 420, 445, etc.

[67]*ConOecDecr*, p. 778. See *ibid* (Trent) p. 636.

Church. The definitions of the Roman pontiff are declared irreformable.[68] Vatican I merits a place among the least reform-minded councils we have surveyed.

The Council is adamant in its conviction that apostolic doctrine has been faithfully transmitted in the Church and adamant in its sense of continuity with the past, even to the point of finding the doctrine of papal infallibility there.[69] At the same time the Council does admit, with all sorts of cautious safeguards, that "growth" and progress" in understanding dogma are possible.[70] In the context of an age fascinated by the idea of organic biological evolution and of the historical progress of the human race, and twenty-five years after the first edition of Newman's *An Essay on the Development of Christian Doctrine*, an ecumenical council for the first time admits that, in some minimal sense, doctrinal development or progress is a possibility. Change, even doctrinal change, might therefore in some form or other legitimately take place.[71]

Vatican II

Vatican II takes more explicit notice of history than any council before it. The Constitution on the Church, though it never loses sight of the transcendent aspect of the Church, insists that the Church truly enters the history of humanity.[72] With Christ described as "the key, center, and end of all human

---

[68] *ConOecDecr*, p. 792.

[69] See *ConOecDecr*, e.g., pp. 782, 788, 789, 791-92.

[70] See *ConOecDecr*, e.g., pp. 785, 787, 792.

[71] *ConOecDecr*, p. 785: "Crescat igitur et multum vehementerque proficiat, tam singulorum, quam omnium, tam unius hominis, quam totius ecclesiae, aetatum ac saeculorum gradibus, intelligentia, scientia, sapientia: sed in suo dumtaxat genere, in eodem scilicet dogmate, eodem sensu, eademque sententia." See nn. 12 and 13 above.

[72] AAS 57 (1965) 14; see also Avery Dulles' observations, *Documents*, p. 11, as well as M.-D. Chenu, O.P., "The History of Salvation and the Historicity of Man in the Renewal of Theology," in *Theology of Renewal* 1: *Renewal of Religious Thought*, 153-66.

history," we discern that the Council is attempting to treat of religious truth in its historical dimension with as much earnestness as had traditionally been applied to its metaphysical dimension.[73]

As in the case of the twenty ecumenical councils which preceded it, Vatican II evidences a strong sense of continuity with the past and a desire to remain true to it. Continuity of faith, spiritual gift, and evangelical tradition from the primitive Church to the present day are often asserted.[74] This is a continuity which even stretches back to Israel and will continue until the end of time.[75] The undeviating nature of the tradition which intervened between the time of the New Testament and the present is confirmed by Vatican II's repeated affirmation of its continuity with previous councils, especially with Trent and Vatican I.[76]

The Council on several occasions makes explicit that the course of the Church's history is under the guidance of Providence.[77] More specifically, the Council employs the Eusebian description of the historical process as a "preparation for the gospel," as an unfolding of a carefully prepared divine plan which presumably enjoys the continuity of beginning, middle, and end.[78] This providential care for the history of the Church in the form of "preparation for the gospel" in the history of Israel climaxed when the gospel was born. The Council recognizes the lifetime of Christ and the period of the apostolic Church as a special moment in its history, and it is to the New Testament, as to the pre-eminent monument of that moment, that recourse must ever be had. It is not without significance that the Council often speaks of antiquity as "venerable."[79]

---

[73]AAS 58 (1966) 1033. See also *ibid.*, p. 1066.

[74]See AAS 57 (1965) 12, 24-25, 27, 39, 44, 55, 58; 58 (1966) 702, 706, 845, 952, etc.

[75]See AAS 57 (1965) 6, 7-8; 58 (1966) 742, 825.

[76]See AAS 54 (1962) 8; 57 (1965) 5, 22, 57; 58 (1966) 727, 817.

[77]AAS 56 (1964) 112; 57 (1965) 28; 58 (1966) 702.

[78]See AAS 57 (1965) 59; 58 (1966) 818, 824, 825. See also *ibid.* 57 (1965) 20; 58 (1966) 948, 950, 1059, as well as *Commentary on the Documents of Vatican II* 3 (ed. Herbert Vorgrimler; New York, 1968) 248-49.

[79]See AAS, e.g., 57 (1965) 28, 76, 78; 58 (1966) 706.

At any rate, along with turning to the past for the content and norm of its present belief and practice. Vatican II invokes "examples" from the past to serve as patterns for the present. History provides material for edification and compelling precedent for present patterns of behavior. Thus, the faithful are to perform the ancient devotional practices in honor of Mary, and the faithful of the Eastern Churches are urged to recite Lauds, *exempla maiorum secuti.*[80] The pre-eminent "example" history provides, of course, is that of Christ Himself, and the Council accordingly encourages the faithful to the "following of Christ."[81]

More than any previous council, Vatican II was aware of change in the world, aware of how the conditions of modern life differed from what went before. There is in the Council a sense of change and a perspective on the temporal order which expressed itself in the forward-looking term "progress." The Council applied this same term to the Church, so that for the first time growth, progress, and development become major conciliar themes. The continuity with the past of which Vatican II was aware was in many instances a developmental continuity, as the Council's appropriation of Eusebius suggests.

The immediate inspiration for the idea of progress is not hard to find. John XXIII's optimistic view of history, which he expounded for the Council on two distinct occasions, could not have failed of effect.[82] More fundamentally, especially over the course of the last century we have learned to think in patterns of progress, evolution, and development, as the Constitution on the Church in the Modern World itself points out.[83] We should not be surprised, therefore, if such patterns are applied to the Church to help explain the phenomenon of change of which the Church had become increasingly aware.

This "progress of the People of God" is sometimes spoken of in just such general terms.[84] At other times it is applied to

[80]AAS 57 (1965) 66, 83. See also *ibid.*, pp. 28, 46, 48, 79; 58 (1966) 692, 709, 1021.

[81]See AAS 57 (1965) 45; 58 (1966) 708, 841.

[82]AAS 54 (1962) 6, 789.

[83]AAS 58 (1966) 1029, 1076.

[84]AAS 58 (1966) 731. See also *ibid.* 57 (1965) 65.

something as specific as liturgical changes or growth in devotion to Mary.[85] But the area to which it is most frequently applied is that of doctrine. Alongside Vatican II's repeated allusions to a progress, evolution, maturation, or growing understanding of doctrine, Vatican I's few lines on the subject seem grudging indeed.[86]

Although "development of doctrine" is a recurring theme of the Council, and although John Courtney Murray once described it as "*the* issue underlying all issues" at Vatican II, the Council gives us very little help in understanding *how* "development" takes place.[87] The old conciliar figure of the Church as the Lord's field practically disappears from the pages of Vatican II, and it is replaced especially by "People of God" and "Mystical Body of Christ." In conjunction with this latter term, we often find the words "increase" and "augment" in the Council's documents, but it is not always easy to specify just what is increasing or augmenting.[88] In the context of the body metaphor, at any rate, the model of organic growth is suggested, and the Council occasionally refers explicitly to the organic nature of the Church's life and constitution.[89] However, the Council never explicitly associates doctrinal development with a model of organic growth.

Vatican II is just as vague concerning the process by which the general "progress" of the Church takes place as it is concerning the "development of doctrine." As a matter of fact, the term "progress" is less frequently used to describe what is happening in the Church than are the traditional descriptions of "renewal," "renovation," and "rejuvenation" (*renovare, instaurare, iuvenescere*).[90] These terms in themselves suggest cyclic or repetitive patterns of history rather than linear progress.

[85]AAS 56 (1964) 106; 57 (1965) 65.

[86]See AAS 57 (1965) 13, 16, 59, 107; 58 (1966) 738, 821, 862, 930, 935, 938-39, 1085.

[87]"This Matter of Religious Freedom," *America* 112 (Jan. 9, 1965) 43 (his italics)

[88]See AAS, e.g., 57 (1965) 11; 58 (1966) 690, 707.

[89]See AAS 57 (1965) 26-27; 58 (1966) 674, 684, 855.

[90]See AAS 56 (1964) 97, 104, 105; 57 (1965) 7, 14, 81, 95; 58 (1966) 703, 704, 713, 739, 1010, etc.

The one traditional term which is practically absent from the Council's document is the word "reform" or "reformation." It occurs only once in connection with the Church.[91] We can only speculate as to the reasons for the avoidance of this term. Its association with Protestantism would possibly be a factor. But perhaps a deeper reason is that, in contrast with the other terms, it connotes a process whereby something is corrected which was wrong. Precisely such an admission the Council makes great effort to avoid, as was dramatically clear in its refusal to admit a real reversal in the Church's teaching on religious liberty and in its well-publicized hesitation to admit guilt in the persecution of the Jews. When the Declaration on Non-Christian Religions asks the Christians and Moslems to heal their dissensions by "forgetting the past," the cynic might well see in this exhortation a convenient solution which the Church is ready to apply to all too many situations.[92] It would seem that however "renovation" or "progress" is to take place, it is not by means of a critical review of past teaching and practice which would clear the way for the future by frankly admitting faults and mistakes.

But such a harsh judgment would not be fully verified in every instance. In the Decree on Religious Life we can find prescriptions for a critical revision (*recognoscere*) of rules, etc.,[93] and in the Constitution on the Liturgy we find similar prescriptions for a revision of the liturgical books in the light of "accurate historical, theological, and pastoral" investigations.[94] It is the Decree on Ecumenism, however, that comes closest to providing for a change *in melius* through recognition

---

[91]AAS 57 (1965) 97. The word "reformation" is used several times in the Council documents with reference to the temporal order: *ibid* 58 (1966) 1085, 1087, 1094, 1105. The Council also repeats the *irreformabilis* of Vatican I concerning papal ex-cathedra pronouncements: *ibid.* 57 (1965) 30. On this problem see Carl E. Braaten, "The Second Vatican Council's Constitution on the Church," *Dialog* 4 (1965) 136-39, esp. 138.

[92]AAS 58 (1966) 742. See the acute observations, esp. on the question of religious liberty, by Lukas Vischer, "The Question of Contradiction and Continuity," *Dialog* 5 (1966) 201-8.

[93]AAS 58 (1966) 704, 705.

[94]AAS 56 (1964) 98, 107, 114, and esp. 106. See also *ibid.* 57 (1965) 57.

of past and present failures. While speaking of faults committed against unity, it on two occasions admits in a generic way that Catholics have to bear their share of the blame.[95] And on two further occasions it calls for "reform." In the first instance "reform" is made synonymous with "renovation," and in context it seems to refer to especially to the personal reform of the individual Christian.[96] The second instance, however, for the first time in a conciliar document since the Council of Basel, clearly speaks of "reform of the Church." It deserves quotation in full:

> Christ summons the Church, as she goes her pilgrim way, to that continual reformation of which she always has need, insofar as she is an institution of men here on earth. Therefore, if the influence of events or of the times has led to deficiencies [*quae minus accurate servata fuerint*] in conduct, in Church discipline, or even in the formulation of doctrine (which must be carefully distinguished from the deposit itself of faith), these should be appropriately rectified at the proper moment.[97]

Several comments are in order concerning the above statement. (1) It is the Church which is to be reformed, not the Christian people. (2) It is a reforming which is ongoing, "continual," so that we can infer that there will never be a time when "conduct, discipline, and doctrine" will arrive at a condition of perfection which will render them "irreformable."[98]

---

[95]AAS 57 (1965) 92-93, 97. See also *ibid.* p. 95, as well as 58 (1966) 938.

[96]AAS 57 (1965) 94.

[97]*Documents*, p. 350; AAS 57 (1965) 96-97: "Ecclesia in via peregrinans vocatur a Christo ad hanc perennem reformationem qua ipsa, qua humanum terrenumque institutum, perpetuo indiget; ita ut si quae, pro rerum temporumque adiunctis, sive in moribus, sive in ecclesiastica disciplina, sive etiam in doctrinae enuntiandae modo— qui ab ipso deposito fidei sedulo distingui debet—minus accurate servata fuerint, opportuno tempore recte debiteque instaurentur." See also *ibid.*, p. 95, and *Commentary on Vatican II* 2, 95-98.

[98]See also AAS 57 (1965) 12, Constitution on the Church: "...Ecclesia in proprio sinu peccatores complectens, sancta simul et semper purificanda, poenitentiam et renovationem continuo prosequitur." See Richard P. McBrien, *Do We Need the Church?* (New York, 1969) pp. 145-48.

(3) Although the phrase *quae minus accurate servata fuerint* is not an overwhelmingly abject admission of fault or mistake, it does form a remarkable contrast with Trent's description of its doctrine of the Eucharist as *omni ex parte perfecta.* (4) The very description of the Church as in pilgrimage suggests the lowly, precarious, and human character of its strivings and hence suggests its need for reform.

This description of the Church as in pilgrimage is closely related to the Council's description of the Church as the "People of God."[99] This is the favorite and characteristic description of the Church in the Dogmatic Constitution on the Church, and it has been interpreted as signifying a breakdown of the old dichotomy between the Church and the Christian people which allowed the Church to be without fault and untouched by history while the Christian people sin and are subject to the "injury of time."[100] The Church truly accepts its historicity and tries to bring its ecclesiology into closer accord with its anthropology. Such an interpretation has a great deal to be said for it, and it contains profound implications for the idea of reform. But the Council nowhere explicitly ratifies such an interpretation, nor does it effectively relate the "People of God" concept to reform of the Church in doctrine and discipline.[101]

Aggiornamento and Historical Consciousness

How can we, therefore, briefly describe Vatican II's *aggiornamento?* We can say that the desire to bring the Church up to date and to make it effective in the contemporary world was the pervasive theme of the Council. Such a desire argues a greater alertness to historical and cultural differences than any

---

[99]See, e.g., AAS 57 (1965) 94; 58 (1966) 938, 1065.

[100]See, e.g., Manfred Hoffmann, "Church and History in Vatican II's Constitution on the Church: A Protestant Perspective," Theological Studies 29 (1968) 191-214, esp. 199-201.

[101]The closest the Council comes is a statement in the Declaration on Religious Liberty, AAS 58 (1966) 938 (Article 12), but the distinction between "People of God" and "Church" is still operative in it.

previous council had shown. In its pervasiveness and implications *aggiornamento* marked a revolutionary shift in reform thinking as religion was changed by and for men in order to accommodate these new historical and cultural differences. In this respect Vatican II stands in marked discontinuity with the councils which preceded it. The fact that the Council fathers spoke of their experience in terms of a new Pentecost suggests some awareness among them that the Council had radical implications.[102] What the Council documents insist upon, however, is that the accommodations which the Council wanted to effect did not change the venerable patrimony of the Christian past, nor did they break the stream of faithful continuity with the apostolic age.

Despite the fact that the Council on several occasions recognized that the world was undergoing dramatic social and cultural transformations, it speaks of its own changes in the reassuring language of adjustment. The very purpose of the changes should be reassuring: they are pastoral in nature, putting the Church at the more effective spiritual and temporal service of the world. Even more reassuring should be the fact that these changes were effected under the providential guidance of the Church's history and as part of the upbuilding and renewal of the Body of Christ or reform of the pilgrim People of God.

The problem with *aggiornamento* as we have just described it is that it fails to provide a solution to the fundamental question which the very word implies: the relationship of the past to the present. Or better, since we do not normally expect a council to provide us with a full-blown theory, we should simply be aware of the fact that Vatican II's *aggiornamento* did not grow out of an understanding of the relationship of past to present which was common to all the fathers of the Council, nor did it project its changes onto a Church which had such a common understanding.

The documents of Vatican II make it perfectly clear that a number of different styles of historical consciousness were operative in the Council, styles not always easily reconcilable with one another. Moreover, the Council failed to take ade-

[102]See, e.g., Butler, "Aggiornamento," p. 6, as well as *AAS* 54 (1962) 13.

quate account of what is most characteristic of contemporary historical thinking, such as the emphasis on discontinuity with the past and the subjectivism resulting from an awareness of the historical conditioning of the historian himself. Thus the relationship of past to present was never resolved. In fact, it was never even raised in a manner to satisfy contemporary thinking on the nature of history. Yet, in this question of the idea of reform, the relationship of past to present is crucial. In the absence of a consistent understanding of it, the Council's fundamental injunction to remain faithful to the authentic past while adjusting to contemporary needs was transformed from a practical norm for reform into an explosive problematic.

At any rate, the basic problem raised by *aggiornamento* will be better understood if we now try to see it as part of a larger pattern. We shall try to describe various styles of reform as they relate to various styles of historical thought or philosophies of history which were operative in the councils and, finally, try to suggest the style of reform thinking which is required by our contemporary historical consciousness.

The first style of historical thinking which we encountered wanted to see the Church as immune to process or to change in doctrine and discipline. The Church moves through history unaffected by history. This style of thinking is sometimes described as "classicism."[103] R. G. Collingwood described it even more aptly as "substantialism" and saw it as the chief defect of Greco-Roman historiography.[104] What it is intent upon is celebrating the voyage through history of some enduring sub-

---

[103]See, e.g., Lonergan, "Existenz," pp. 247-48, and John Courtney Murray, S.J., "The Problem of Religious Freedom," *Theological Studies* 25 (1964) 560. Practically the same thing is meant by the "two-story" or the "ontocratic" view of the universe. See, e.g., George A. Lindbeck, "A Protestant Point of View [on *Lumen gentium*]," in *Vatican II* (n. 1 above) pp. 220-21, and Josef Smolik and the Concilium General Secretariat, "Revolution and Desacralization," *Concilium* 47 (1969) 175-76.

[104]*The Idea of History* (New York, 1956) pp. 42-45. For a more detailed study of historical thinking in antiquity, which emphasizes its variety and especially the awareness of progress, change, and discontinuity in many sources, see Ludwig Edelstein, *The Idea of Progress in Classical Antiquity* (Baltimore, 1967).

stance which is really untouched by history. Rome, for instance, was such a substance for Livy. In conciliar terms, the unchanging substance of the Church is clearly distinguished from the contingencies which affect at least some of its members. This style does not admit that change exists except in the form of certain external challenges to the existence of the substance. These challenges could conceivably destroy the substance, but they cannot intrinsically modify or change it.

In the case of the Church, heretics or evil custom have been such challenges. The Church's duty in these cases is to excise or "uproot" them, so that the Church can continue its course through history. The purpose of such doctrinal and moral reform is not change, but to preserve from change a substance which really should not be subject to change in the first place. If the Church is conceived principally as a doctrinal society, doctrine is the primary object of such protection. This style of historical thinking can perhaps best be described as metaphysical, i.e., not historical at all.

In the early Christian era substantialistic historical thinking itself underwent a significant change when it confronted the idea of a providential guidance of the course of events.[105] Eusebius' *Praeparatio evangelica* would be an example of this style. Although the idea of a providence guiding history tolerated and perhaps even suggested the idea of development and stages or periods in a master plan, it had a large dose of substantialism in it as it was actually practiced, especially as substantialistic thinking related to the enduring character of Christian dogma, moral teaching, and the structure of ecclesiastical government.

What was the characteristic of this providentialism in the Middle Ages was that it made God the principal agent in history.[106] Man proposed but God disposed. Thus what happened in the past was endowed with a superhuman and even sacred quality. If the earlier substantialistic historical thinking

---

[105]See Collingwood, *Idea of History*, pp. 46-56. See also, e.g., Pelikan, *Historical Theology*, p. 7, on the "progress in religion," i.e., growth without change, in Vincent of Lerins.

[106]See Collingwood, *Idea of History*, pp. 48, 55.

was incapable of recognizing change, providential thinking made legitimate change the work of God alone. Any change introduced by man was sacrilegious. True reform, therefore, consisted in removing threats to the sacred. Men were to be changed by religion, not religion by men. Whatever human element was recognized in the past tended to be identified with what was strictly accidental. It was an appendage, an external dressing, which could be modified or adjusted in the case of *urgens necessitas vel evidens utilitas*. What was permissible was "emendation," to use the word of Constantinople I and of John XXIII. This emendation could take the form of modification of something already in existence, or even the introduction of something new, e.g., a new regulation or penalty, especially if thereby an old custom or discipline would be reinforced. But the sacred patrimony was to be kept untouched. Metaphysical thinking now combined with metahistorical thinking.

Sacred metahistory could easily incorporate into itself the Roman idea, notably revived in the Renaissance, that history was nothing else than philosophy teaching by example, especially moral example.[107] History in this view has an ethical, edifying, or exhortatory purpose. The record of the past was viewed as a storehouse of *exempla* from which one drew prescriptive patterns of action which were directly transferable to the present situation. If the lives of illustrious orators and statesmen were examples to be imitated, how much more worthy of imitation were the examples of the saints and especially of the Saint of saints! The behavioral patterns of the sacred past were under the special guidance of providence and therefore provided models of behavior which were beyond criticism.

What is common to all three styles of historical thinking we have been describing is their minimal awareness of change, especially of change in the sense of the "new." This does not mean that change had not taken place. It simply means that

---

[107]See Gilmore, *Humanists and Jurists*, pp. 14-37, and esp. George H. Nadel, "Philosophy of History before Historicism," in *Studies in the Philosophy of History* (ed. George H. Nadel; New York, 1965) pp. 49-73.

men did not have the perspectives to recognize it as having taken place. The result was that the past was seen, not on its own terms, but exclusively according to the realities of the present. That is why medieval Englishmen, Frenchmen, and Germans thought they were Romans.[108] No change, therefore, was desirable or necessary in the present, for none had taken place in the past.

There was another style of antique thinking which did recognize change, but it was change in the form of decline from an earlier and better state or condition. This style is generally described as "primitivism."[109] The idea of such a decline or fall was expressed in the story of Adam and Eve as well as in Hesiod's myth of the golden age. Conciliar documents suggest an earlier period of Christianity as the golden age, which by its presumed purity stands as a norm, model, and ideal for all that follows. Reform is effected by a return to it. Despite what we might think at first glance, primitivism can be reconciled with the other forms of historical thinking we have described. The decline can be restricted to just one aspect of reality, such as morals, or it can be applied to "men" as distinct from the divine society to which they belong. As applied to Christianity in the later Middle Ages, it was precisely these adaptations which at times primitivism underwent.[110]

The style of reform which is appropriate to primitivism is "rejuvenation," "revival," "rebirth," and even "reform" itself. This style of historical thinking recognizes change for the

---

[108]See Burke, *Renaissance Sense of the Past*, esp. 6, 18-20, and J. M. Wallace-Hadrill, *The Barbarian West: The Early Middle Ages* (New York, 1962) p. 146. See also Edmund Schlink, "A Protestant View of the Vatican Council Schema *De ecclesia,*" *Dialog* 3 (1964) 140.

[109]See Arthur O. Lovejoy and George Boas, *Primitivism and Related Ideas in Antiquity* (New York, 1965) esp. pp. 1-102, as well as, e.g., George Boas, *Essays on Primitivism and Related Ideas in the Middle Ages* (Baltimore, 1948); Mircea Eliade, *Cosmos and History: The Myth of the Eternal Return* (New York, 1959) esp. pp. 112-30; Jürgen Moltmann, *Religion, Revolution, and the Future* (New York, 1969) esp. pp. 21-25; Harry Levin, *The Myth of the Golden Age in the Renaissance* (Bloomington, Ind., 1969); and my article, "Fulfillment of the Christian Golden Age under Pope Julius II," *Traditio* 25 (1969) 265-338.

[110]See, e.g., my *Giles of Viterbo*, esp. pp. 108, 179-91, and Bouwsma, "Three Types of Historiography," pp. 306-9.

worse, a decline from an earlier and presumably normative state or condition. It was in the context of a secularized application of this style that the idea of a "renaissance" of arts and literature was born in Italy in the fourteenth and fifteenth centuries. Reform consists, therefore, in breathing new life into what has wilted, in healing what is sick, in reconstructing what has disappeared. The pattern of history, if it is not to be utterly pessimistic, is cyclic or repetitive, and it looks to the past for its substance and norms.[111]

What distinguishes decline-history from the others we have seen is that it takes account of change. It realizes that the present is different from the past. Thus it has a sense of distance from the past and a perspective on it. The late Erwin Panofsky noted how the sense of historical perspective influenced painting and sculpture during the Renaissance: medieval artists who worked from literary sources dressed ancient gods or heroes in medieval costumes, whereas the Renaissance recognized that such a procedure was not "historically true."[112] Between the times of the Romans and the present there was an intervening something, a "middle age," which was different. To recover the Roman past, Renaissance men realized they had to leap over what had intervened. In other words, what was gradually dawning was a sense of discontinuity in history.

As was mentioned earlier, the first Protestants exploited this discovery of discontinuity to the disadvantage of their Catholic counterparts. The Catholics were often willing to acknowledge a discontinuity in the standard of moral behavior in the Church, but not in its enduring substance. Both parties, in any case, looked backwards to the early Church as to a period of special purity in doctrine and morals.[113] What especially distinguished Catholics from Protestants was their belief that the intervening tradition was continuous, homogeneous,

---

[111]See Burke, *Renaissance Sense of the Past*, pp. 87-89.

[112]*Renaissance and Renascences in Western Art* (New York, 1969) esp. pp. 42-113. See also Gilmore, *Humanists and Jurists*, pp. 9-10.

[113]See, e.g., Calvin and Sadoleto, *Reformation Debate*; John P. Dolan, *History of the Reformation* (New York, 1967) esp. p. 26; John M. Headley, *Luther's View of Church History* (New Haven, 1963) esp. pp. 162-94.

undeviating, and therefore just as "venerable" as the early Church itself.

The Enlightenment threw history's goal into the future and gave nineteenth-century historiography its orientation towards "progress."[114] The philosophers and historians of this period accepted the idea of change, of discernible and coherent pattern, and of golden age. They transformed these ideas by secularizing them and by turning them around to make them forward-looking. In searching for models to explain progress, they easily turned in the nineteenth century to ideas of evolution and organic growth.[115] They were thus able to explain both change and continuity. The present was still found in the past. The present was the best explanation of the past, for it showed where the past was naturally tending all the time.

The most distinguished and sophisticated Catholic work of the nineteenth century which shows the influence of this style of thinking was Newman's *Essay on the Development of Christian Doctrine*. Present reality is the term towards which earlier reality naturally tended. According to at least one critic of Newman, entelechy is the key to his system: "a thing's true nature is best revealed in its later history and final state: in becoming a butterfly the chrysalis becomes itself."[116] Authentic change is never by way of reversal, but only by way of further development of the already existing.[117] Doctrinal reform is by way of growth or accretion, never by way of rejection of what has gone before. In the early years of the present century such thinking had a natural affinity for the conception of the Church as the Mystical Body of Christ, which was then gaining prominence and which continued to dominate Catholic thinking on

[114]See John Edward Sullivan, *Prophets of the West* (New York, 1970) pp. 21-87.

[115]See e.g., Sullivan, *Prophets*, pp. 79, 86, and Wilson H. Coates and Hayden V. White, *An Intellectual History of Western Europe* 2: *The Ordeal of Liberal Humanism* (New York, 1970) 133-68.

[116]Anthony A. Stephenson, S.J., "Cardinal Newman and the Development of Doctrine," *Journal of Ecumenical Studies* 3 (1966) 467. See John Henry Newman, *An Essay on the Development of Christian Doctrine* (Garden City, N.Y., 1960) pp. e.g., 121, 135, 164.

[117]See Jaroslav Pelikan, *Development of Christian Doctrine: Some Historical Prolegomena* (New Haven, 1969) p. 145. See also Butler, "Aggiornamento," p. 11.

the nature of the Church until the very eve of Vatican II.[118]

In summary, we can say that we have seen a number of styles of historical thought which have conditioned the idea of reform as we have known it in the past. These styles all appear or are suggested in the documents of Vatican II. What all these "philosophies of history" have in common is that they are traditional or conservative as regards the past. We can list, for instance, five reform procedures which such styles of thinking allow: (1) reform by excision or suppression (keep what you have by removing threats to it); (2) reform by addition or accretion (keep what you have untouched, but add new things alongside it); (3) reform by revival (keep what you have by breathing new life into it); (4) reform by accommodation (keep what you have by making adjustments for differences in times and places); (5) reform by development (keep what you have, but let it expand and mature to its final perfection). What is notably absent from this listing, of course, is reform by transformation or even by revolution, for both of these imply at least a partial rejection of the past in the hope of creating something new. In practice, Vatican II's *aggiornamento* has been just such a transformational or revolutionary reform. But much of our present confusion concerning it is due to the fact that we have not as yet explicitly related this transformational or revolutionary practice to an adequate contemporary philosophy of history.

Contemporary Historical Consciousness

The possibility of the "new" has been opened up by modern historical consciousness.[119] This is the style of historical thinking which has its remote origins in the Renaissance discovery of discontinuity, but whose implications are being worked out

---

[118]See Hoffmann, "Church and History," pp. 195-98.

[119]See, e.g., Giulio Girardi, S.D.B., "The Philosophy of Revolution and Atheism," *Concilium* 36 (1968) 109-22, esp. 118.

only in our own day. Its immediate academic history, therefore, stretches from von Ranke or Dilthey to the present. Hence it is associated with the elusive problematic known as historicism, even though it is by no means identified with it.[120] There has, of course, been considerable disagreement even among historians about the implications of modern historical method and historical consciousness. Today, however, perhaps enough convergence of views has taken place to allow us to speak of some of them compositely as a "contemporary philosophy of history." Since some understanding of this philosophy is essential to our topic, I shall attempt a brief description of what seems to me characteristic of it.[121]

Contemporary philosophy of history is based upon one fundamental presupposition: history as a *human* phenomenon. By history is meant both past reality as it actually happened and the reconstruction or understanding of that reality as it takes place in the historian's mind and imagination. Contemporary philosophy of history labors to explore the implications of this fundamental presupposition.

What are some of these implications? First, the scope of the historian's inquiry, insofar as he is a historian, is the past *as human*, i.e., the past as it resulted from human passions, decisions, and actions. This means that for the historian the past is radically contingent and particular. Just as each person is

---

[120]On historicism see Sullivan, *Prophets*, pp. 89-162; H. P. Rickman's "General Introduction" to Wilhelm Dilthey, *Pattern and Meaning in History* (ed. H. P. Rickman; New York, 1961) pp. 11-63; Hajo Holborn, "Wilhelm Dilthey and the Critique of Historical Reason," in *European Intellectual History since Darwin and Marx* (ed. W. Warren Wagar; New York, 1966) pp. 56-88; Arnaldo Momigliano, *Studies in Historiography* (New York, 1966) pp. 105-11, 221-38; John Cobb, "Towards a Displacement of Historicism and Positivism," *Concilium* 57 (1970) 33-41.

[121]The description is my own synthesis of what I believe the best contemporary thinkers are saying about history and method, as this is verified in my personal experience and reflections as a historian. I refer the reader especially to Hans-Georg Gadamer, *Le problème de la conscience historique* (Louvain-Paris, 1963); H. Stuart Hughes, *History as Art and Science* (New York, 1964); Wolfhart Pannenberg, "Hermeneutics and Universal History," in Wolfhart Pannenberg *et al., History and Hermeneutic* (New York, 1967) pp. 122-52; Richard E. Palmer, *Hermeneutics: Interpretation Theory in Schleiermacher, Dilthey, Heidegger, and Gadamer* (Evanston, Ill., 1969), as well as Collingwood, *Idea of History*, and Leon J. Goldstein, "Collingwood's Theory of Historical Knowing," *History and Theory* 9 (1970) 3-36.

different from every other, so is each event, each culture. In this sense history can never repeat itself, for the same contingent concatenation of human factors can never be reassembled. Each word, document, event is historically and culturally conditioned, radically individualized, and understandable as history only insofar as it is unique and the result of man's more or less free action and decision.

The result of this approach to the past is that it is desacralized. Events are seen as the result of human and contingent causes, not as the result of divine interventions. If you will, the past is "deprovidentialized," as every effort is made to explain it as the result of human and earthly factors. God may have hardened Pharaoh's heart, but the historian is interested only in the contingent social, economic, and psychological factors which were at work on Pharaoh. These factors, as the results of human passion and decision, inject discontinuity into history; for man is capable of reversing himself, or changing direction, and thus of being discontinuous with himself.

The historian, accordingly, becomes deeply aware of the discontinuity in the past, and he is forced to remove from his consideration any overarching divine plan. Indeed, historicism was born out of disillusionment with attempts to discover and expose such plans either in their sacral or secularized forms.[122] The past is human. This means it is to be understood in terms of man, who is free and contingent and who has not masterminded a coherent pattern for the history of his race. Biological models for man's course through time are just as inappropriate as elaborate metaphysical ones. They imply that whatever is new in the present is simply the natural unfolding of the potential of the past. They make inadequate allowance for human freedom. In philosophy of history as well as ecclesiology, we must bring our theory into agreement with our anthropology. Evolutionary progress is an inappropriate postulate; for it hypostasizes history apart from man, who is capable of reversing himself.

---

[122]See, e.g., Rickman's "General Introduction" to Dilthey's *Pattern and Meaning*, pp. 25-26.

What modern historical method enables us to understand more clearly than was ever understood before, therefore, is that every person, event, and document of the past is the product of very specific and unrepeatable contingencies. These persons, events, and documents are thus contained within very definite historical limits. By refusing to consider them as products of providence or as inevitable links in a preordained chain of historical progress, decline, or development, we deprive them of all absolute character. We relativize them.

The importance of such relativization is clear when we consider the alternative. If a reality of the past is not culturally relative, it is culturally absolute. It is sacred and humanly unconditioned. There is no possibility of a critical review of it which will release the present from its authoritative grasp. Contemporary philosophy of history relativizes the past and thus neutralizes it.

What this means is that we are freed from the past. We are free to appropriate what we find helpful and to reject what we find harmful. We realize, perhaps to our dismay, that we cannot simply repeat the answers of the past, for the whole situation is different. The question is different. We are different.

The historian's realization that he is different from previous generations is simply a further ramification of his realization of man's radical historicity. What the contemporary historian is very much aware of is that he himself is *in* history and cannot step outside it as he searches the past. He himself is culturally conditioned. He does not bring pure intellect to his research. He brings a mind filled with questions, methods, prejudices, and personal quirks which are the result of his own personal cultural and psychological history. History in the sense of human understanding of the past is thus further relativized—relativized by the contingency of the historian's own understanding.

The contemporary historian, therefore, cannot subscribe to the crude objectivism of his predecessors, as expressed, for instance, by von Ranke. *Wie es eigentlich gewesen* is beyond his grasp. This means that the definition of what an "authentic" interpretation of the past is must be considerably relativized too. To speak of it as something that intelligence and good will can capture in its entirety and articulate once and for all is to remove authenticity from the realm of human capabilities. A further element of discontinuity is thereby injected into our understanding of the past. Not only has the past been removed from some superplan, but it also is now subject to the discontinuity of insight which will be operative between one historian and another or between one generation and another. Thus we can with truth speak of a "changing" or even a "new" past.

Finally, the great cultural repercussion of contemporary historical thinking is the realization that, if the past imposes no pattern upon us, we are free to try to create the future. Our freedom is, of course, limited. The fact still remains, however, that if we are freed from the past in the sense of not expecting it to tell us what to do, we are free to make our own decisions for the future. Indeed, we have no escape from such freedom, fraught as it is with dreadful burdens.

Historical Consciousness and Reform

What remains to be done is to examine what "contemporary historical consciousness," i.e., the realization of man's radical historicity, means for the problem of reform. In the first place, if we are to think rationally about reform, we must "demythologize" our style of historical thinking. Our consciousness must be purified of "substantialism," "primitivism," etc. When I say we should purify our understanding, I do not mean we should jettison the truth which these forms of historical thinking tried to express but could do so only in an unhistorical way. For instance, what is common to all these earlier approaches to history is their emphasis on historical continuity. The fact is that there *is* a strong continuity in history, whether we are speaking of history as past human reality itself or as historians' understanding of the past reality. As regards the latter, there are at least three sources for continuity: (1) continuity of the documentary evidence, e.g., the primary documents for any Christian reform, the Word of God as contained in the canonical Scriptures, are now textually verified and major textual changes seem most unlikely; the hard core of data in these documents acts upon the scholar and thereby imposes limits upon "interpretation," i.e., upon discontinuity; (2) continuity deriving from the fact that the basic operations of the human mind do not radically change from culture to culture; (3) continuity of "tradition," i.e., the historians are produced by an earlier generation of historians and hence are culturally linked to them; this is the other side of the fact that the historian himself cannot step outside of history. What is to be corrected in Catholic reform thought, therefore, is the exclusiveness of its emphasis on continuity.[123] With such an exaggerated emphasis as we had had until now, we have been inhibited from undertaking a really critical review of the past so that a new break for the future could logically be opened up.[124]

A critical review of the past implies at least the possibility of rejecting the past, i.e., of acknowledging that there were certain realities *quae minus accurate servata fuerint*. It seems to me that such an acknowledgement is permissible if we correctly make use of contemporary philosophy of history. In the first place, the philosophy denies entelechy as a reliable principle of interpretation. An institution or an idea could have developed otherwise, for it is the product of human and contingent causes. To reply that providence ordained such a development simply removes the institution or idea from the area of human examination and hence silences both the historian and the theologian. If some given historical reality *could* have developed

---

[123]This particularly Catholic tendency to refuse to recognize the discontinuities in history is being increasingly criticized. See Vischer, "Contradiction and Continuity;" Hoffmann, "Church and History"; and Francis Oakley, *Council over Pope* (New York, 1969), where the refusal to admit radical discontinuities in history is described as "a classic Catholic stratagem," p. 134. Bernard J. F. Lonergan, S.J., ascribes much of the blame for "the present [unsatisfactory] situation in the Church" to the Catholic "classicist" mentality: "The Response of the Jesuit, as Priest and Apostle, in the Modern World," Vol. 2, no. 3 of *Studies in the Spirituality of Jesuits* (St. Louis, 1970) 105. In this connection see AAS 58 (1966) 1077, Decree on the Church in the Modern World.

[124]See, e.g., Leonard Swidler, "What Can History Do for the Church?" *Journal of Ecumenical Studies* 4 (1967) 128-32, and F. Houtart and F. Hambye, "The Socio-Political Implications of Vatican Council II," *Concilium* 36 (1968) esp. 91-92.

otherwise, and if we are still human agents operating in *human* history, we are free to change and even to reverse the direction of that reality if we so choose. What I am talking about, of course, is revolution, a term which historians use to describe certain phenomena which have occurred in the Church but which ecclesiastical documents never employ except in a pejorative sense.

In the second place, the contemporary historian realizes that data is subject to many "interpretations." That is, different scholars and different ages will have different questions encased in different presuppositions to address to the data. Therefore, they will evoke from the data different answers. What we are doing, obviously, is divesting the very concept of "authenticity" of a rigidly objective character. When Vatican II enjoined upon religious orders that they should follow the "mind of the founder," the supposition seemed to be that there was one authentic expression of that mind which could be discovered once and for all and then be adjusted to today's needs.[125] Such an approach to authenticity needs to be tempered by at least two considerations. First, although we hope for an ever more accurate understanding of the past as we labor for it in research and discussion, we realize we shall never fully appropriate any past reality in its totality and on its own terms. No insight will perfectly exhaust the data's intelligibility, most especially if the "data" is God's self-communication in revelation. Any authenticity, therefore, is at least somewhat partial and incomplete. Unlike Trent, we realize that our authenticity will not be *omni ex parte perfecta*. Secondly, we realize that authenticity is not perfectly distinct from relevancy. The only meaningful questions we can ask the past are ones which are somehow relevant to our own needs and interests, and these needs and interests vary with different individuals, generations, and cultures.[126] As Michel de Certeau observed a few years ago, "En changeant, nous changeons le passé."[127]

---

[125]See AAS 58 (1966) 988, as well as 703, 711, etc.

[126]The Council itself touched on this question, AAS 57 (1965) 103; 58 (1966) 823-24.

[127]"L'Epreuve du temps," *Christus* 13 (July, 1966) 314.

We are thus brought to the final implication that contemporary philosophy of history has for reform. It teaches us that we must create the future.[128] In other words, it forces upon us the realization that, in the case of Christian reform, understanding of the past, howsoever authentic it might be, is not enough. Reform is also a practical matter. It requires not only understanding but also a translation of understanding into reality through our powers of imagination and creativity.

Imagination and creativity must enter every reform if it is not to be utterly irrelevant and dreary beyond human endurance. As a matter of fact, creativity has been at the heart of every successful reform and renaissance, even when people sincerely believed that they were doing nothing else than transposing the past into the present.[129] Creativity, which is radically opposed to slavish imitation, implies both utilization of the past and rejection of the past. The outcome of creativity, in any case, is something *new*.

We have seen that we have to allow for a considerable difference of emphasis in our "authentic" insights into the past. Even greater variety will surface when it comes to the question of translating insight into action, i.e., of producing that creative transformation which is genuine reform. At this juncture what is required is decision. What is required is to choose one or other practical course of action, after respective merits have been reviewed. What is not required is further reflection provoked by the misapprehension that, because a variety of options is offered as "authentic," "*the* true mind" has not as yet been discovered.

The *aggiornamento* of Vatican II was our starting point. What I have tried to show is that, in the context of the philosophies of history upon which it seems to have rested, it is an

---

[128]Man's power over the future and his responsibility towards it is pivotal, for instance, in Teilhard de Chardin's understanding of history. See Piet Smulders, S.J., "Teilhard and the Future of Faith," *Theology Digest* 27 (1969) 327-37, esp. 330-31.

[129]Examples of such a misapprehension on the part of reformers are not hard to find. One of the best in ecclesiastical history is certainly the case of Pope Gregory VII, whose reform began the transformation of the papacy into the centralized monarchy which has perdured to our own day. See, e.g., Brian Tierney, *The Crisis of Church and State, 1050-1300* (Englewood Cliffs, N.J.,1964) esp. pp. 47-48.

inadequate expression of what is required today and, indeed, of what is actually happening today. We are not experiencing a "reform" as that term is traditionally understood as a correction, or revival, or development, or even updating. We are experiencing a transformation.

As we are all keenly aware, such a transformation raises immense practical and theoretical questions. This article certainly did not intend to satisfy these questions except by helping to clarify one aspect of the relationship of past to present and future. What we tried to do was to put the question of Christian reform into the context of various philosophies of history which have conditioned it in the past, and then to suggest how the problematic changes if reform is put into the context of contemporary philosophy of history. Such philosophy helps us to interpret more accurately what is happening. At least it should disabuse us of the illusion that the past will tell us what to do and that we do not have to be as decisive and creative as our Christian predecessors were. In fact, we should be even more decisive and creative. To a degree inconceivable to previous generations of Catholics, we realize that such a decision and creativity, with its heavy responsibilities, is required. We have a new understanding of what we are, beings of radical historicity. This new understanding of ourselves imposes upon us a new way of thinking and acting about "reform."

5

Developments, Reforms, and Two Great Reformations: Towards a Historical Assessment of Vatican II

Questions about the significance of Vatican II exercise us today as urgently as they did while the Council was in session.[1] These questions are often addressed to historians. The familiar evasion that it is too soon to judge is not without merit, but it also risks relegating the historical profession to irrelevance for the contemporary life of the Church.[2] It was for this reason that I attempted some years ago to venture an assessment of the Council, and I would now like to take up the subject again, but from a different point of view.[3] The present article presupposes the earlier one and builds upon it.

[1]The problem appears in many forms. See, e.g., Andrew M. Greeley, "The Failures of Vatican II after Twenty Years," *America* 146, no. 5 (Feb 6, 1982) 86-89, and the various responses in the same journal, 146, no. 23 (June 12, 1982) 454-61; Antonio Acerbi, "Receiving Vatican II in a Changed Historical Context," in *Where Does the Church Stand?*, Concilium 146 (1981) 77-84; Alberto Abelli, "Ein Grundgesetz der Restauration? Zum Entwurf einer 'Lex fundamentalis' der Kirche," *Herder Korrespondenz* 33 (1979) 36-43; Karl Rahner, "Towards a Fundamental Theological Interpretation of Vatican II," *TS* 40 (1979) 716-27; various authors, "Vatican II 20 Years Later," *National Catholic Reporter* 18, no. 44 (Oct. 8, 1982); William Mc-Sweeney, *Roman Catholicism: The Search for Relevance* (New York: St. Martin's Press, 1980).

[2]On this issue see my "Church History in the Service of the Church," *America* 147, no. 10 (Oct. 9, 1982) 188-90.

[3]"Reform, Historical Consciousness, and Vatican II's Aggiornamento," *TS* 32 (1971) 573-601, reprinted above.

In that earlier article I stated: "In the breadth of its applications and in the depths of its implications, *aggiornamento* was a revolution in the history of the idea of reform."[4] I still stand by that judgment. The question today, however, is not whether "the idea" of *aggiornamento* was revolutionary but whether the applications and implications of the idea are correspondingly being translated into action. Is a "revolution" taking place, or did Catholicism simply indulge in a momentary flirtation or infatuation with an idea? How much and how deeply have things changed? What kind of "reform" did the council initiate, and how can its magnitude, or finitude, be assessed? These are the questions that seem to be on many people's minds.

There can be no doubt, of course, that the Council effected some change. We worship and pray differently. Our official stance towards other religious bodies is different. We must reckon with the inescapably obvious phenomenon of change in a Church that previously boasted that it did not change. But now we ask how these changes are being "received" and whether we are slipping back into previous patterns, invoking the documents of the Council to ratify the *status quo ante*. Are the changes that the Council promoted to be interpreted in some minimal or some maximal sense? These are simply other ways of posing the sames questions as above, but they have the advantage of highlighting the most incontestable feature of any "reform" or "reformation": its claim to effect change.

Today no one with even the slightest knowledge about the history of the Christian Church denies that it has during its long course in this world undergone a number of significant changes—in its organization, in the styles of its theology, in the forms of its piety, in the ways it exercises its ministries. From a theological viewpoint one could postulate that this phenomenon of change is implied in the very incarnational or historical nature of Christianity. Change does not, therefore, jeopardize a deeper identity; it is, rather, the precondition for maintaining the authenticity of that identity. These postulates or their equivalents seem to have undergirded, in any case,

4Above, p. 48.

every reform or reformation the Christian tradition has known. In this article I shall simply take them for granted and limit my task here to categorizing, analyzing, and even quantifying the forms in which change has taken place. With that task accomplished, we will still not be able perfectly to assess Vatican II, but we shall have moved "towards an assessment," which is all that I—or any historian at this stage—can hope to achieve.

I believe that if we look at the history of Christianity, we can see change taking place in three general ways. I will use the terms "developments," "reforms," and "reformations" to denote those ways. The meanings I give the terms are my own. The methodology I use in arriving at them is vaguely inspired by the work of Erwin Panofsky,[5] Crane Brinton,[6] Ian Barbour,[7] and Thomas Kuhn,[8] who applied similar approaches to quite different historical phenomena. I am aware of the pitfalls of these approaches and the criticisms their creators received, but at present I know of no better way of going about the project I have undertaken. I take full responsibility for the method, and I do not ask any of the distinguished historians I have cited to assume responsibility for what, in the final analysis, is a way of looking at the phenomenon of change in the Church that is personal to me.

My documentation, moreover, will be small because the issues are big. This is not a sly way of saying "trust me," but a straightforward admission that my theses cannot be strictly proved. I am engaged in a historical essay, with all the cautions for the reader that such an enterprise entails.

First, then, a definition of terms. By "developments" I mean

[5] *Renaissance and Renascences in Western Art* (New York: Harper and Row, 1960).

[6] *The Anatomy of Revolution* (rev. ed.; Englewood Cliffs: Prentice-Hall, 1952).

[7] *Myths, Models, and Paradigms: A Comparative Study in Science and Religion* (New York: Harper and Row, 1974).

[8] *The Structure of Scientific Revolutions* (2nd ed.; Chicago: University of Chicago, 1970). The book has been the subject of an immense amount of discussion and controversy. See, e.g., David A. Hollinger, "T.S. Kuhn's Theory of Science and Its Implications for History," *American Historical Review* 78 (1973) 370-93; and Garry Gutting, ed., *Paradigms and Revolutions* (Notre Dame: University of Notre Dame, 1980).

all those changes, some of them of vast proportions, that have occurred in the Church without being deliberately and self-consciously initiated by Church leadership for the good of the Church. This lack of original self-determination is what, in this definition, distinguishes "developments" from both "reforms" and "reformations." Developments are changes in mentality or structures that occur in tandem with realities located "outside" the Church, often by a kind of osmosis with them. So gradual and unobtrusive at times is their impact that they may only with the benefit of considerable hindsight be recognized as even having taken place. Once recognized, however, as affecting the Church, some developments have been repudiated as abuses, whereas others have been ratified and embraced. Only upon recognition, if it ever occurs, might developments therefore begin to assume some characteristics of reform or reformation.

Examples of developments abound. One of the earliest and most striking was the change in cultural framework that early Christianity underwent as it was gradually and more effectively assimilated into the Hellenistic world. The "gospel" may or may not have been "Hellenized," but it surely began to be conceptualized and articulated in a different cultural framework than that of Jesus the Jew.

Constantine issued his edict of toleration without the organized initiative of Church membership, yet momentous changes resulted for the Church. Later, the conversion of the barbarian tribes resulted in the phenomenon known as the Feudal Church. Then the revival of urban life in the eleventh and twelfth centuries and the establishment of universities in the thirteenth effected other changes. The invention of printing and, almost in our own day, the invention of radio and television supply examples of further changes that took place "outside" the Church but that have affected it. The evolving role of women in modern society is another such development, as is the emergence of democracy as a characteristic political form of many modern states.

There are, however, other changes that came about in a different way, changes that were self-consciously initiated by membership within the Church for the presumed good of the

Church, changes *in melius*. This is the common characteristic of what I mean by both "reform" and "reformation," and that is how those terms are generally understood by historians.[9] It can effectively be argued that none of these self-conscious phenomena, no matter how important they may have been, brought about such profound changes as did some of the developments I mentioned. Be that as it may, "reforms" and "reformations" have been a significant feature of Church history, especially in the West since the eleventh century, and the very presupposition that underlay them—that the Church has the right, and sometimes the duty, to initiate changes within itself—is a fact of great importance. In any case, it is somewhere within these two categories that Vatican II must be located; for, whatever else it did, it surely undertook its task of *aggiornamento* in a fully self-conscious way.

How do I distinguish reform from reformation? Here I am dependent upon Thomas Kuhn. By "reform" I mean simply all those changes enacted within the Church that take place within a given frame of reference. They are changes within a system. They are "adjustments" or "emendations," terms sometimes used to describe what Vatican II was all about.[10] They do not require or effect a new "myth," "model," "universe of discourse," or a new "paradigm." In fact, they support or further articulate certain unchallenged assumptions within a given system. They do not rock the boat; they steady it on its course.

Some examples will perhaps clarify what I mean. The decree *Omnis utriusque sexus* of the Fourth Lateran Council, 1215,

---

[9]One of the first to study the phenomenon was Yves M.-J. Congar, *Vraie et fausse réforme dans l'église* (Paris: Cerf, 1950). For further bibliography see my "Reform, Historical Consciousness" p. 44, nn. 1 and 2. To these listings should now be added other works such as Giuseppe Alberigo, "'Rèforme' en tant que critère de l'histoire de l'église," *Revue d'histoire ecclésiastique* 76 (1981) 72-81; Marc Venard, "Réforme, Réformation, Préréforme, Contre-Réforme: Etude de vocabulaire chez les historiens récents de la langue française," in *Historiographie de la Réforme*, ed. Philippe Joutard (Paris: Delachaux & Niestlé, 1977) 352-65. See also, along a slightly different line, my "Catholic Reform," in *Reformation Europe: A Guide to Research*, ed., Steven Ozment (St. Louis: Center for Reformation Research, 1982) 297-319.

[10]See my "Reform, Historical Consciousness" above p. 48.

required annual confession and Communion during the Easter season of every adult Christian. This was a reforming decree, and an important one at that. Yet it did not shock the system. It built on a pattern of piety already recognized as normative, and it confirmed a sacramental practice and theology that were not contested. No matter how effectively or ineffectively the decree was implemented, there is no record of formal or organized opposition to it.

The Council of Trent insisted on the duty of bishops to reside in their dioceses. The Council almost destroyed itself in the bitter debate over whether this duty was *jure divino* or *jure humano*, but there was no serious question that this was a duty to be insisted upon. It was a decree, moreover, meant to strengthen a system already normatively in place, not to dislodge it with a new one.

The approbation given the mendicant orders like the Dominicans and Franciscans in the thirteenth century began to alter the way religious life was conceived and practised in the Church. These approvals practically for the first time officially invested religious with the care of souls. The recurring conflicts that the mendicants had with the bishops through most of the Late Middle Ages indicate that certain old prerogatives were challenged, and a new, parallel system of ministry had come into being as a result of initiatives within the Church.

Nonetheless, it can be argued that this change was simply an adjustment in a system in which monks had, in fact, engaged in ministry of both word and sacrament, though that ministry was at times officially denied them.[11] Bitter though the conflicts between the mendicants and the bishops were at times, the status of the mendicants does not seem to represent an across-the-board shift in ministerial or ecclesiological paradigm. My very hesitancy in pronouncing in this case indicates, however, that in practice it may sometimes be difficult to distinguish between "reform" and "reformation."

---

[11]See canon 16 of Lateran Council I, 1123, in *Conciliorum oecumenicorum decreta*, ed. Giuseppe Alberigo *et al.* (2nd ed.; Rome: Herder, 1962) 169.

What, then, do I mean by "reformation"? I mean a self-consciously induced change in ecclesiastical life or consciousness that is based on principles that tend to dislodge old ones. This reorientation implies, in Kuhn's term, a paradigm shift. It is *not* "puzzle solving" or "mopping up." It means the displacement of one inclusive model or even world view for another. When Copernican astronomy replaced Ptolemaic, to use one of Kuhn's examples, it created a different way of viewing the universe and did not merely effect an adjustment within a prevailing view. It forced the abandonment of certain basic assumptions and it replaced them with new ones.

The difficulties in applying such a construct to the history of Christianity are even more enormous than those in applying it to the history of science. For believing Christians, for instance, a total shift of paradigm is by definition impossible. Moreover, the charting of changes in assumptions and in consequent practice in a reality as sprawling as the history of Christianity, or even in a single moment of it, is fraught with problems of which the appearance of a new scientific theory, usually in the mind of one individual, is innocent. Nonetheless, it seems to me that enough can be salvaged in the construct to allow it to be of some use to us in the task in which we are engaged. The difficulties should not, however, be minimized.

There is no doubt, in any case, that some of the proposed or even actualized changes that have occurred in Christian history were of far greater import than others, and that we fail to understand them if we in unreflective manner equate them with lesser ones. Some changes do not merely confirm and further elaborate received ideas and institutions; they challenge and contradict them. They originate from different presuppositions. To understand Luther's conflict with the Catholic Church, the comparison of his doctrine of "justification by faith alone" with the teaching of the Council of Trent on that same issue is only a first step. The inquiry will be hopelessly superficial unless it goes further. That doctrine is the tip of a *different* iceberg.[12]

[12]See, e.g., my "Erasmus and Luther: Continuity and Discontinuity as Key to Their Conflict," *The Sixteenth Century Journal* 5/2 (1974) 47-65, now reprinted in my *Rome and the Renaissance* (London: Variorum, 1981) XII.

Are there in the long history of Christianity any phenomena of self-consciously induced changes that qualify as "reformations"—or, to be slightly safer, as "*great* reformation"? In my opinion, there are two: the so-called Gregorian Reform of the eleventh century and the Lutheran Reformation of the sixteenth. It is by an analysis of them that I intend to move "towards a historical assessment of Vatican II," in order to judge whether that Council better fits the category of "reform" or "reformation." I will try to isolate and analyze features in the two reformations that made them successful and thereby try to construct an "anatomy" or a "structure" of an ecclesiastical reformation.

By a "successful reformation" I mean merely that, within the limits of all historical endeavors, the change was able to institutionalize itself in such an effective fashion that it wrought a transformation in ways of thinking and behaving that had extremely long-range effects. By "success" I mean, therefore, that the change was clearly identifiable as relating to the impulse that initiated it, that it clearly displaced or notably modified older institutions, that it created mechanisms and agents to perpetuate itself so that a reversal of course would for a long period of time be virtually impossible. By "success" I do not mean to pass judgment on any of the other merits or demerits of the phenomena in question.

I
The Gregorian and Lutheran Reformations

Before I proceed to an analysis of these two movements, some background information may be helpful. I assume that the readers of this volume will have sufficient familiarity with the Lutheran Reformation to follow my arguments, but perhaps some basic facts about the Gregorian Reform—or Investiture Controversy, as it is sometimes termed—may need to be recalled.[13] That phenomenon was a complex series of historical

---

[13]Handy summaries of the issues involved and the assessments of various historians, with bibliography, are provided in Schafer Williams, ed., *The Gregorian Epoch:*

events that in its more obvious phase stretched from the beginning of the pontificate of Leo IX in 1049 to the Concordat of Worms in 1122. Its most intense period was the pontificate of Pope Gregory VII, 1073-86. Gregory's conflict with Emperor Henry IV of Germany led to civil war in Germany, to the siege and sacking of Rome by imperial and Norman forces and to the death of the pope in exile.

The "reform party" (the popes and their supporters from 1049 to 1122) fought for the elimination of simony, clerical concubinage, and lay intervention in the designation of bishops, including the bishop of Rome. These were its immediate goals. But since it thereby challenged the feudal and familial relationships between the clergy and lay magnates upon which early medieval society rested, historians see the controversy as the first massive attack on the feudal system as such. It is generally considered one of the great turning points of Western history.

Within the Church itself the Gregorian Reform insisted on clearer distinctions of function between clergy and laity. It based its case on ancient canons and secured its position through an unprecedentedly heavy reliance on legalistic argumentation. It sparked the development of a more visible, vigilant, and centralized papacy, more conscious than ever before of a pre-eminence over other bishoprics. Papal right to act in various civil and ecclesiastical cases began to be exercised with new frequency and with a clearer sense of ultimate authority. The movement thus had an effect on the way the Church functioned that would long outlast the achievement of its more immediate goals over which the struggle raged until at least 1122. In fact, the role of the papacy in the Church and the dominant, almost exclusive role played by the clergy in Church

Reformation, Revolution, Reaction?[1] (Lexington, Mass.: Heath, 1964), and Karl F. Morrison, ed., *The Investiture Controversy: Issues, Ideals, and Results* (New York: Holt, Rinehart and Winston, 1971). The bibliography is immense. The classic study is Augustin Fliche, *La Réforme grégorienne* (3 vols.; Louvain and Paris: Champion, 1924-37), and there is a sober account in Hubert Jedin, ed., *Handbook of Church History* 3 (Montreal: Palm, 1969) 351-465. The most recent presentation is Uta-Renate Blumenthal, *Die Investiturstreit* (Stuttgart: Kohlhammer, 1982).

order, as we know these realities today, are clearly traceable to the Gregorian Reform.

A word must be said, meanwhile, about my isolating the specifically Lutheran component in the much larger phenomenon of the Protestant Reformation. I do so for reason of economy in an essay that in fact demands several volumes to argue its case effectively, and also because Luther was the catalyst who unleashed the larger reality that always remained somewhat dependent on the direction he gave it, immense though the diversities within the reality would be. Whatever those diversities, for instance, there was in every case a clear rejection of the papal component in Church order. Luther is, in other words, prototypical as the initiator of the various Protestant reformations, and I employ him in the essay in precisely that role; implied, therefore, is a regrettable but necessary oversimplification of the situation that developed in the sixteenth century to a large extent as a result of his initiative.

We are now, at last, in a position to study these two "great reformations." In what follows I propose four major aspects under which to view and compare them. The first question to be answered here is how these reformations verify in their content my claim for their paradigmatic radicality. Next the language or "rhetoric" will be examined, to see how these reformations made themselves heard and had impact on consciousness. Thirdly, I will examine the quality of leadership in both of them and, finally, try to see ways they grounded themselves in social or politico-ecclesiastical institutions.

I have created these four categories of analysis, along with their subdivisions, during the years I have spent teaching and writing about reforms and reformers in the Church. The categories are my own. Except for the idea of "model" or "paradigm," I am not aware of any immediate dependencies on other authors for them, although at this point I would have difficulty in retrieving the various works that over a long period of time may have suggested one or another of them to me. I believe they are adequate to the task I have set, but of course others could be added to them for a more complete treatment.

Their principal advantage, it seems to me, is that they lift our considerations to a broad perspective. In this they differ from sociological studies of the Council that view it close-up and that examine more immediate phenomena like the impact the Council has thus far had on religious vocations, attendance at Mass, and similar issues. Helpful though such approaches are, they need to be supplemented with perceptions of longer range. That is what I attempt here.

The Content and Paradigm

1) *A focused issue.* Both reformations centered their attention on a single problem, the remedy of which would set things right. Although the Gregorians for the first several decades tried to deal with various problems like simony and clerical celibacy, as well as the regulation of episcopal elections, Gregory VII by 1075 joined battle with the emperor over the issue of lay investiture, i.e., the conferral on prelates by members of the laity of the insignia for their spiritual office. This practice symbolized for the Gregorians lay control of episcopal nominations. That was the "abuse" that sparked the dramatic clash and consequently it became focus and symbol for all the other issues the reformation carried with it.

Luther arrived at his central issue more quickly and directly. True, the controversy exploded in late 1517 over the preaching of indulgences by Johannes Tetzel, but already underlying the Ninety-five Theses was the doctrine of "justification by faith alone," even if the clarifying experience of the *Turmerlebnis* had not yet taken place, as some scholars maintain. Luther eloquently stated his position on that central doctrine in his *Freedom of the Christian*, addressed to Pope Leo X in 1520, and for him that doctrine remained the fundamental plank in what came to be a program, however unsystematically presented that program always remained.[14]

---

[14]There are so many studies of Luther's theology that it would be impossible here to list even the most important ones. I will content myself, therefore, with naming three comprehensive works that are often cited and are easily available: Gordon Rupp, *The Righteousness of God: Luther Studies* (London: Hodder and Stoughton, 1953); Paul Althaus, *The Theology of Martin Luther* (Philadelphia: Fortress, 1966); and Gerhard

2) *Tests for authenticity.* The psychological advantages of a central issue, clearly focused, are many. Proponents are better able, for instance, to "prove" its authenticity. For the proponents, their position thus becomes incontestable, easily defended against the attacks of opponents. The Gregorians found their justification in the canons, some authentic and some inauthentic.[15] The canons represented, quite literally, the "truth," whereas the contemporary practice of investiture was merely "custom."[16] That practice, judged against the canons, came to be seen as *perverted* custom, an unwarranted "development." The canons acted as a first principle, as a norm not itself requiring authentication but that whereby all other norms were authenticated. Retrieved from the hallowed past, the canons passed judgment on the present but were not themselves susceptible of judgment.

Luther's test was even more fundamental. His doctrine of justification encapsulated "the gospel." He retrieved the doctrine, fallen into desuetude in his own day and even suppressed by the papacy, from St. Paul, who articulated it in unmistakably clear terms in Roman and Galatians. These two epistles became for Luther the heart of "the canon within the canon," against which the rest of the Bible was judged. The doctrine was the essence of Christianity, clear and incontestable. The fact that the doctrine contradicted common sense and the fallacies of human philosophy, i.e., Aristotle, only validated its divine origins in "Scripture alone."

3) *Programs.* What is remarkable about the focused issues in both these cases is that they implied the basis for broad

Ebeling, *Luther: An Introduction to His Thought* (Philadelphia: Fortress, 1964). See also Jack Bigane and Kenneth Hagen, *Annotated Bibliography of Luther Studies, 1967-76* (St. Louis: Center for Reformation Research, 1977). Still useful for Catholics approaching Luther is Jared Wicks, ed., *Catholic Scholars Dialogue with Luther* (Chicago: Loyola University, 1970); see also Wicks's article on Luther in the *Dictionnaire de spiritualité* 9 (1976) 1206-43. A recent work especially pertinent to this article is Yves Congar, *Martin Luther: Sa foi, sa réforme* (Paris: Cerf, 1983).

[15]An important work indicating the centrality of the canonical revival in the Gregorian Reform is John Joseph Ryan, *Saint Peter Damiani and His Canonical Sources* (Toronto: Pontifical Institute of Mediaeval Studies, 1956).

[16]See Gerhart B. Ladner, "Two Gregorian Letters: On the Sources and Nature of Gregory VII's Reform Ideology," *Studi Gregoriani* 5 (1956) 221-42.

programs of change. Viewed clinically and abstractly, this need not have been true. Neither of the issues, for instance, was exactly new to Christianity. But imbedded as they were in specific historical circumstances and in the personalities of their proponents, they assumed radical implications as they were translated into action. They became the foundations from which their proponents intended to accomplish their divinely ordained task of setting the world right.

To insure the universal observance of clerical celibacy, the elimination of simony in the "buying and selling" of Church offices, and the establishment of canonical procedures in the election of bishops, the Gregorians in effect began to create a new Church order. With the advantages of hindsight, we today see more clearly where their proposals were carrying them than they did themselves. The Gregorians set in motion a long process that would eventually eliminate from Church order the active role the lay magnates had played for centuries. Canon law, interpreted in a decidedly papal sense, would soon emerge as the central ecclesiastical discipline. Most important of all, the papacy emerged with new or at least more vigorous claims, so that the leadership and effective mechanisms in Church order passed from abbots, bishops, and lay princes to the popes. From the shadowy, ill-defined, principally symbolic and liturgical role of the popes in previous centuries, the "papal monarchy" came into being. By the early fourteenth century, the curial theologian Giles of Rome could utter a definition of ecclesiastical order that would never have crossed the mind of anybody in the tenth: "the pope, who can be said to be the Church."[17] That was a hotly contested proposition even when Giles advocated it, but the fact that it even occurred to him tells us much about the shift in consciousness that had occurred in the intervening centuries in some theologians, partisan advocates though they may have been.

Luther passed rather quickly from a focused issue—an abstract and strictly theological one at that—to an across-the-board program. Earlier in the same year in which he wrote the

[17]See Yves Congar, *L'Eglise: De saint Augustin à l'époque moderne* (Paris: Cerf, 1970) 272-73.

Freedom of the Christian, he published his *Appeal to the German Nobility*. In some ways that document reads like nothing more than a grocery list of late-medieval grievances and thus would seem to contain nothing new. Read in the context of Luther's other writings and in the context of his doctrine of justification, the document has an internal cohesion that, again, sets the stage for a radical change in Church order. It would cancel or blunt, for instance, many of the achievements of the Gregorians regarding the role of laity and papacy in the Church.

Underlying his writings on an even deeper level was a redefinition of piety and religious attitude. His shorthand expression for this redefinition was a rejection of "works righteousness" in favor of righteousness by faith. Along this line he composed a new sacramental theology and constructed a powerful theology of the Word. In all this he was convinced he was ultimately basing himself on the traditional repudiation by the Church of Pelagianism, the damnable heresy that the doctrine of justification by faith laid low.

4) *Paradigm shift.* In each of these cases the programs were unacceptable and even unintelligible to outsiders, and they soon provoked stubborn opposition. The opposition originated not because one or other of the ideas or changes was in itself unthinkable, but because all the elements were related to one another to form a program or system, though this fact may sometimes have been only vaguely intuited rather than clearly perceived. More fundamentally, the system itself rested on new presuppositions. A paradigm shift had occurred.

From at least the sixth to the eleventh century, the Church in the Latin West operated on a lumbering basis of ill-defined exercise of authority. This situation reflected and was part of the "medieval muddle" known as feudalism. Put more positively, authority in Church and society was seized and exercised as needs emerged. Undifferentiated function was the operative pattern for ecclesiastical and secular leadership. Bishops and great abbots, who were often members of the local nobility, performed functions that we would today unhesitatingly describe as civic or political; conversely, lay magnates and kings sometimes convoked and almost invariably implemented synods, and they considered it their right in most cases to have a determining voice in the nomination of prelates. Emperor Henry III exercised this last prerogative, with beneficial effects, for the bishopric of Rome just a few decades before the conflict broke out between his son and Pope Gregory VII. The decree of the Roman Synod of 1059, promoted by the papal reform party later known as the Gregorians, that placed the election of the pope in the hands of the cardinal-bishops, was an affront to this practice and a harbinger of things to come.

From a religious point of view, there were certainly problems with some of the practices that prevailed in the Feudal Church. Unworthy men became bishops and abbots, sometimes through deals that deserve the label of simony that the Gregorians attached to them. But there were also advantages for the Church. Dedicated prelates, for instance, were not a rarity. In any case, it never occurred to most persons that the practices were "abuses." Those practices simply were the way things were. For the Gregorians to make their case credible, they had to introduce a new way of arguing, based on a new model of the ideal Church.

"Scripture alone" is a theological principle found in Aquinas.[18] But the circumstances surrounding Luther's invocation of it invest it with a quite different significance. He certainly was not in the first place opposing Scripture to "tradition," as Catholics sometimes assume, but to "philosophy." The *scriptural* doctrine of justification contradicts *Aristotle's* proposition that it is by doing good deeds that one acquires good habits and thus becomes a good person. For Luther, the Christian is good only through divine favor—"grace alone"— not by his deeds or good works. This truth destroys the pretensions of human reason.

Luther came to oppose the papacy and the Church order that the papacy symbolized, therefore, not so much because he found no basis for it in Scripture but because the papacy, in opposing his teaching on justification, in effect was suppres-

---

[18] *Sum. theol.* 1, 1, 8, ad 2.

sing the gospel. It was for this reason that he saw it as the Antichrist, busy in the world doing the the devil's work for him.

With that fact as background, Luther could invoke the "Scripture alone" principle in a different way—now to search the Bible for a Church order that in his opinion more clearly conformed to the Bible, shorn of the accretion of the centuries that had intervened since then. Calvin and other Protestant leaders would carry this search much further. With "Scripture alone" as his professed norm, Luther applied it to sacramental practice and theology, and to other issues as well. Luther's repudiation of canon law (mere "human inventions") as a basis for that order was as fervid as the Gregorians' advocacy of it.

In a role reversal with the papal party of the Gregorians, the "papists" now had to argue for the validity of the *status quo*. The problems that "the Lutherans" and "the papists" had in understanding each other was now not only the vast range of particulars over which they were in controversy, but the difference in the underlying models, values, authenticity tests, and presuppositions that were explicitly or implicitly in play. A paradigm shift had taken place concerning what the Church and even the "true Christian" looked like.

Reform Rhetoric

It is one thing to have a program based on a paradigm shift; it is quite another to rally support for it. Paradigm shifts by definition fly in the face of common sense and received opinions. To the unbiased beholder they are far from self-validating. They threaten the very basis on which institutions are seen to operate, and thus seem to be nightmares rather than solutions.

Certainly, the societies to which they were addressed had to be to some extent psychologically and sociologically disposed, and some sense of anomaly within the old paradigm had to be operative. In both of our instances, grievances and problems of various kinds were surfacing and beginning to be addressed in more effective fashion. These grievances and problems were the soft underbellies of the old paradigm, but the radical surgery that a new paradigm implies is always an unpopular intervention.

The new paradigms had to be mounted, therefore, in a propaganda campaign as massive as the radicality of the program itself. Both these reformations forged in fact, without the considered calculation with which we are familiar today, effective instruments for such a campaign.[19] Their rhetoric outfitted their paradigms with emotional and valuational overtones.

1) *Slogans.* First, in each case a slogan soon emerged. For the Gregorians the slogan was the "the liberty of the Church." This is what they convinced themselves they were fighting for when they opposed the emperor and other lay leaders. For Luther the slogan was "justification by faith alone" or simply "the gospel." These words were not invented by Luther, but he invested them with a meaning peculiarly his own.

The psychological advantages of such condensed and encapsulating expressions need not be proved to persons like ourselves, so familiar with the techniques of modern advertising. Slogans function as cheer, as loyalty test, as battle cry. In the eleventh and twelfth centuries the slogan of the Gregorians seems to have performed all these functions. Luther, with his usual psychological acumen, actually saw his message as a "battle cry."[20] The success of the Gregorians in making their slogan operative could not be more effectively demonstrated than by its eventual incorporation into the prayers of the liturgy.[21] It was thereby both enshrined and also provided with an ongoing mechanism with which to perpetuate the vision of the Church that it represented.

[19]See, e.g., a recent study of visual propaganda: R. W. Scribner, *For the Sake of Simple Folk: Popular Propaganda for the German Reformation* (Cambridge: Cambridge University, 1981).

[20]"Preface to the New Testament," in *Martin Luther: Selections from His Writings,* ed. John Dillenberger (Garden City, N.Y.: Doubleday, 1961) 15.

[21]Oratio," in *Missale Romanum,* May 25, feast of St. Gregory VII: "Deus, in te sperantium fortitudo, qui beatum Gregorium confessorem tuum atque pontificem, pro tuenda Ecclesiae libertate...."

It is important to note the relationship of these two slogans to the focused issues that characterized each of the reformations. The advantages of such focuses are many: they give the movement a center, enable friends to be distinguished from enemies, provide a measure with which to distinguish progress from regress. And, critically important, they can be summed up in a slogan.

An example of a reform that in its articulation lacked such focus is the Council of Constance, 1414-17, which called for "reform in faith and morals, in head and members." A potentially more radical program is difficult to imagine. But its very all-inclusiveness, reflected in the slogan, helped dissipate, rather than marshal, reform efforts in Europe in the century before the Reformation. It did, nonetheless, engender part of that vague sense of anomaly, that unease with the present dispensation, that was a precondition for receptivity to messages like Luther's.

2) *Redefinition.* One of the most striking features of these two reformations is that they were unanticipated in the forms in which they received their classical articulation. There was relatively little in the history of the Middle Ages until about 1050 that suggested that the "liberty of the Church" from lay interventions was a possible or desirable "reform." The role that emperors, kings, and nobles played was generally perceived as good, not bad—as indispensable for the smooth functioning of Church and society. The Gregorians redefined this role when they opposed the "truth" of ancient canons to the mere "custom" of their contemporaries. In this dramatic redefinition we have another indication of the revolutionary nature of that reformation.

Although the century between the end of the Council of Constance and publication of the Ninety-five Theses resounded with cries for reform, nobody anticipated that "justification by faith" would be the issue over which conflict would explode. Eminent spokesmen for reform like Erasmus called for simplification of religious practices and for greater interiority— for a more spiritual appreciation of "good works." No one questioned, however, that "good works" were "good" and religiously meritorious. Nonetheless, Luther effected precisely such a reversal, such a turnaround, through his presentation of the truth of "justification by faith alone." This doctrine was framed in Luther's "theology of the cross," which would lead him to defend the proposition that naturally good acts are sins.[22]

The very boldness of these redefinitions gave them rhetorical force. They could not be ignored, for they flew too clearly in the face of common sense. They could not get lost in a bundle of other, more conventional proposals, for they challenged too directly the very foundations on which the other proposals rested. Doubters could be referred to clearly designated tests for their authenticity.

What I am saying is that in both of these reformations "abuses" were not abuses until they were perceived and defined as such. Until that moment they were good, or at least neutral. From the psychological standpoint, it is difficult to conceive a more brilliant success than the redefinitions these reformations articulated.[23]

3) *Prophetic stance.* Another feature of this reform rhetoric was the prophetic stance and language assumed by the two leaders. This language was "prophetic" in at least four senses. First, the style resembled the assertive, take-it-or-leave-it style often assumed by the prophets of Israel. Put negatively, it eschewed discursive, dialectical, homiletical, or persuasional styles. Gregory VII, moreover, quoted the prophets and knew that it was incumbent upon him to "cry aloud."[24] Luther, the "doctor hyperbolicus," insisted that a proclamatory and categorical style, "assertion," is what the Christian message by its very nature requires.[25]

[22]See Dillenberger, *Luther* 501 (WA 1, 353), Heidelberg Disputation: "3. Opera hominum ut semper sint speciosa bonaque videantur, probabile tamen est ea esse peccata mortalia."

[23]See, e.g., the section on "persuasive definitions" in Charles L. Stevenson, *Ethics and Language* (New Haven: Yale University, 1944) 206-26.

[24]See *The Correspondence of Pope Gregory VII,* ed. and tr. Ephraim Emerton (New York: Norton, 1969) 8, 11, 15, 17, 32-33, etc.

[25]See especially his reply to Erasmus entitled *On the Bondage of the Will,* in Luther and Erasmus: *Free Will and Salvation,* ed. and tr. E. Gordon Rupp (Library of Christian Classics 17; Philadelphia: Westminster, 1969) 105-12 (WA 18, 603-8).

Second, both men assumed the burden of denouncing the evils of their day, cost what it might. This meant unmasking the enemies of truth and confronting them with their error. They were both convinced they lived in a world in which the devil held sway.[26] In this dangerous situation enemies assumed a bigger-than-life stature. They had to be unmasked for what they were, and the dangers they posed unambiguously denounced. This is the "rhetoric of reproach" in which both reformers consistently indulged.[27]

While they did this, they assumed a further prophetic function of holding out the promise of better times to come, once truth triumphed over error. Even as they "tore down" one order, they promised to "build up" another. It must be admitted that the good measure of pessimism in both Gregory and Luther somewhat inhibited this aspect of their prophetic function. Nonetheless, along with a "rhetoric of reproach," they utilized a "rhetoric of great expectations." Along with enemies to be destroyed, there were hopes to be realized. Thus was created a *vision* that goes beyond a "program." Such rhetoric minimizes difficulties, creates enthusiasm, discourages sober analysis.

Finally, and perhaps most importantly, both men assumed the persona of a prophet. According to the prophetic model, they identified their cause with God's. Although they understood the term in quite different ways, both men were preoccupied with *justitia*—justice, righteousness, God's sovereignty. In the earliest interpretation of Luther by his followers, he was in fact perceived as a prophet, after centuries of prophetic silence among God's people.[28] Both men, surely, saw themselves as spokesmen for God, the essential definition of the prophetic role.

[26]For Gregory see *Correspondence*, e.g., 11, 12, 51, 92, 100-101, 103, 123, 150, 161, 162, 172, 179, 189-90, 195; for Luther see Hans-Martin Barth, *Der Teufel und Jesus Christus in der Theologie Martin Luthers* (Göttingen: Vandenhoeck und Ruprecht, 1967), and Heiko A. Oberman, *Luther: Mensch zwischen Gott und Teufel* (Berlin: Severin und Siedler, 1982).

[27]On "rhetoric of reproach" and its relationship to reform, see my "Historical Thought and the Reform Crisis of the Early Sixteenth Century," *TS* 28 (1967) 531-48.

[28]See John P. Dolan, *History of the Reformation* (New York: New American Library, 1967) 21-24.

The net result of the prophetic stance is that it provokes a crisis situation. By definition given to confrontation, it forces decision. It divides father from son and mother from daughter. Both the Gregorian and the Lutheran reformations convulsed the society of their day; they led to war, bloodshed, and political disarray. The emperor ordered Gregory to descend from the papal throne, denouncing him to the whole Christian world as "false monk" and not a true pope, and he eventually was responsible for Gregory's being driven from the city of Rome and dying in desperate exile. Luther lived his whole life after 1521 as an excommunicate and an outlaw of the Empire, who most surely would have been put to death if he had not been in the protective custody of powerful political allies.

The crisis that the Gregorians provoked in Western society ended with a kind of reconciliation, though so shaky that it contained a potential for a later schism if the memories of the role played by lay leaders in the Church were ever later revived and fanned into flames, as happened in the sixteenth century. Luther's crisis produced an immediate schism, resulted in a century of religious wars throughout northern Europe, and divided Western Christianity until our own day.

Leadership

A feature that characterized both reformations, as must be clear by now, was the fierce passion that animated both Gregory and Luther. Although Gregory was involved in the movement almost from the beginning, the reformation was under way before he clearly assumed its direction. Nonetheless, he soon made the reformation *his* reformation. He identified it with the very meaning of his life itself. It today quite correctly bears his name.

Luther, on the other hand, was the pivotal figure from the very first. It was his case and his cause that stood in the dock. For his truth he risked his reputation and his life—over the course of decades. With excellent psychological accuracy statements are ascribed to both men that vindicate their utter commitment to their causes: to Gregory, as his dying words, "I have loved justice and hated iniquity; therefore I die in exile;" to Luther, "Here I stand; I can do no other."[29]

The importance of such utter commitment in effecting a reformation is obvious. Reformation means a changing of set ways and mentalities, which implies dislodging imbedded interest-groups and earning their hatred. The resistance to such change is inevitably enormous and requires heroic energies to overcome it. The old axiom that it is more difficult to reform a religious order than to found a new one betrays a profound understanding of how institutions function.

If historians find it difficult to chart the precise impact of reform councils like Lateran IV and Constance, part of that difficulty lies in the fact that these councils, being the responsibility of everyone, ended by being the responsibility of no one. The permanent impact that Trent had upon the Church was due to the fact that in the end the Council, whose major effort was to strengthen episcopal authority and pastoral care, in effect handed over its own implementation to the papacy. Without precisely intending to do so, the Council in the end thus strengthened the papacy and helped it continue along Gregorian lines.

The impact of Trent was also due to the devoted follow-through of people like Charles Borromeo and others, who appropriated with zeal specific proposals and were determined to perpetuate them through institutional forms like seminaries, frequent diocesan and provincial synods, enforced residency of pastors in their parishes, and clear pastoral directives. Borromeo's bitter conflicts with the Spanish authorities in Milan testify to the risks he was prepared to take to see his measures implemented.

---

[29]See, e.g., Paul Egon Hübinger, *Die letzten Worte Papst Gregors VII.* (Opladen: Westdeutscher Verlag, 1973). The eight personal traits that Ann Ruth Willner identifies in the charismatically effective political leader are clearly and to a high degree verified in both Gregory and Luther: *Charismatic Political Leadership: A Theory* (Princeton: Princeton University, 1968).

Institutional Grounding

In both the Gregorian and Lutheran reformations, leadership of course extended beyond the two principal figures. Others were won to the cause, and they committed themselves and their fate to its furtherance. Thus these movements began to insert themselves into the fabric of society, with the effect that some old institutions began to function in different ways and some new institutions, self-perpetuating in certain instances, were founded.

The papal Curia, for example, had a long history before the Gregorians came onto the scene, yet that reformation gave great impetus to its fuller development and imbued it with a keener sense of responsibility as an authoritative clearinghouse with an international scope. The intestate clergy that celibacy implied must also enter into consideration. In Germany in the sixteenth century, the Protestant princes who seized Church lands or who particularly enjoyed the role Luther sometimes assigned them as "emergency bishops" soon had high stakes in the outcome of the religious controversies. We assume that, as reformers, Gregory and Luther had a powerful impact upon the religious sensibilities of Christians who heard their message. I mention the Curia, intestate clergy, and the German nobility, however, to underscore that the message had an institutional component as well.

Further examples of institutional influence could be adduced, but I will limit myself to one for each case: for the Gregorians, the creation of the college of cardinals, and for the Lutherans, the married clergy. It seems to me—although I am not aware that other scholars have argued in precisely this way—that both movements thus created a new "class" of Church officers or ministers whose self-interest, even survival, was essentially tied to the success of the respective reformations.[30] In both cases the new class of officers or ministers became important agents for the implementation of the reformation.

[30]Steven Ozment touches on this issue in his *When Fathers Ruled: Family Life in Reformation Europe* (Cambridge: Harvard University, 1983).

The Gregorians redefined the function of the cardinals of the Roman Church, transforming an essentially liturgical and politically inert group of clergy into one of the most powerful forces in Europe by placing the election of the pope in its hands, from whose membership in the future most popes would be selected. It is true that for centuries to come the history of the sacred college was tortured, tumultuous, and ambivalent. Nonetheless, the important fact is that out of the Gregorian reformation emerged a new body, inserted into the very fabric of Church order, whose meaning and immense prerogatives were created and consolidated in the course of that reformation.

The Gregorians early on deliberately created their institution, though with no clear sense of its ultimate significance. Luther was anything but an organizer, and the "reformed Church" that came into being under his leadership was for years seriously disturbed by his failure, for instance, to provide clear guidelines about how the rights and obligations of bishops and princes were to be delimited. He created at the outset, however, a new clergy.

The doctrinal convictions and the liturgical practices of that clergy distinguished it from its Catholic counterpart. But what irrevocably tied this clergy to Luther's reformation, I suggest, was the permission to marry. It was this fact that made it a new institution. That institution thus had both human and divine obligations to wife and to children. It seems to me that, with Luther's justification of marriage for the clergy and with Catholicism's adamant refusal to countenance that change, a new class came into being, now bound to the reformation by irreversible choice of the married state. Thus Luther created, somewhat unwittingly, a self-perpetuating instrument to carry forward his vision and program. Whereas the election decree of 1059 that placed the election of the pope in the hands of the cardinal bishops was directly related to the objectives the Gregorians had in mind, married clergy was only a distant corollary to Luther's central concerns. Nonetheless, with it an institution came into being upon whose viability the permanent viability of this reformation to a large extent depended. A significant change had been effected in society at large that grounded the reformation. Without such groundings, programs of reformation tend to remain imprisoned in the minds, hearts, and words of those who conceive them, without final insertion into the societies they are intent upon reforming.

II
Vatican Council II

By this time I trust that I have provided sufficient information to indicate why both the Gregorian and the Lutheran movements deserve the appellation "great reformation" that I attach to them, as well as how and why they deserve to be judged "successful." By means of their content, rhetoric, leadership, and institutional grounding, they proposed and effected a paradigmatic change that had long-range effects. We are now in a position to address Vatican II in this large historical perspective. In the light of the categories I have utilized, does it more closely approximate a "reform" or a "great reformation"? How does it relate to "developments"?

The disclaimer that it is too early to judge must, of course, be invoked. After all, it took centuries for the implications of the Gregorian reformation to take hold and become widely operative. We must expect the same of Vatican II, if it is to be categorized as "great reformation." Nonetheless, we at least have at our disposal some categories of analysis and some historical models against which to test what we have experienced and observed over the past twenty years. In my opinion, there is reason to believe that in Vatican II we may indeed be witnessing another "great reformation." That is the central statement in my thesis. However, there are such notable discrepancies between Vatican II and the two models—especially in the rhetoric, leadership, and institutional grounding of the Council—that a definitive judgment is at this point impossible. Even so, by engaging in this process of assessment, tentative though it is, we are enabled to get a helpful perspective on the Council and thus on ourselves. That last is the ultimate objective, I believe, of good historical studies.

The Content and Paradigm

In my earlier article I proposed that in effect Vatican II created a new ecclesiological paradigm. The Council never unambiguously articulated that paradigm, however, and hence any discussion of it will to some degree reflect the lack of clarity in the conciliar statements themselves. In what follows concerning Vatican II, in *all* its aspects, I will try to follow Aristotle's sage advice of not forcing more clarity and precision onto this subject than it from its nature will bear.[31] I would maintain, nonetheless, that in both its formal and its material aspects the idea of *aggiornamento* marked a notable departure from the fundamental paradigm of Church order that prevailed before the Council.

Viewed formally, in the breadth of its application and in the depth of its implications, *aggiornamento* was a revolution in the history of the idea of reform. This was—and remains— my fundamental judgment about the Council. I will not repeat here all the arguments for that judgment that I originally adduced, but merely state its premises.

Until the Council, Catholic thought on reform was based on what can be called a "classicist" mentality. According to such a mentality, the Church moved through history more or less unaffected by history. "Men must be changed by religion, not religion by men" was the concise articulation of this position, enunciated by Giles of Viterbo at the opening session of the Fifth Lateran Council, 1512.[32] The Church was so aware of the divine origin of its doctrines, rites, and discipline and of the continuity of its traditions that the historical and contingent components of these realities received relatively little attention.

In the past hundred years especially, a new "historical consciousness" has emerged in Western society that has influenced even sacred studies—Scripture, liturgy, canon law, the "de-

---

[31] *Nicomachean Ethics* 1, 3, 1-4.

[32] Mansi 32, 669: "Homines per sacra immutari fas est, non sacra per homines." See my *Giles of Viterbo on Church and Reform* (Leiden: Brill, 1968) esp. 179-91.

velopment" of doctrine. The "progressive" theologians who eventually came to have such great influence at Vatican II were affected by this mentality, and they soon began to determine the way the Council conceived its task. An awareness, more radical than ever before in the history of the Church, that "things have not always been thus" took hold, and it emboldened the Council to review its agenda with new eyes.

The Council never denied, of course, the divine origin of the message and mission of the Church; in fact, it insisted upon it repeatedly. Nevertheless, the Council also evinced a sense of freedom and flexibility in its interpretation of the tradition of the Church that was unprecedented. Thus it arrived at the basic intuition underlying *aggiornamento* that, with all sorts of qualifications, religion had to change to meet "the needs of the times." That intuition constitutes the formal element of *aggiornamento* that is new in the history of the idea of reform and reformation, and it notably modifies the axiom of Giles of Viterbo.

The Council thereby began to effect a shift in consciouness closer to a "great reformation" than to a "reform." The seeds for this "revolution" are contained in the way the idea of *aggiornamento* began to operate within the Council, bursting the modest confines originally foreseen for it. The fact that the Council was at the time hailed as "the end of the Constantinian era," the "end of the Counter Reformation," and even as the "new Pentecost" testifies that participants and observers sensed that something more momentous was at stake than adjustments or emendations within a given system.[33] The ship was not perceived as being steadied in its course but as striking out in a new direction.

What was that new direction? Here we begin to enter the material aspects of the paradigm. Unlike its formal character, the content of the paradigm cannot be summarized in a few paragraphs. The situation is due in part to the vastness and diffuse character of the conciliar documents, in part to the fact

---

[33]See, e.g., Congar, *Luther* 79, and Christopher Butler, "The *Aggiornamento* of Vatican II," in *Vatican II: An Interfaith Appraisal*, ed. John H. Miller (Notre Dame: University of Notre Dame, 1966) 6, as well as *AAS* 54 (1962) 13.

that the Council generally did not state where and to what degree its directives differed from those in force before the Council. Broad aims did emerge, however, and taken together they indicate the changes in substance that the paradigm began to effect.

Put in the most generic terms, the aims of the Council were as follows: to end the stance of cultural isolation that the Church was now seen as having maintained; to initiate a new freedom of expression and action within the Church that certain Vatican institutions were now interpreted as having previously curtailed; to distribute more broadly the exercise of pastoral authority, especially by strengthening the role of the episcopacy and local churches vis-à-vis the Holy See; to modify in people's consciousness and in the actual functioning of the Church the predominantly clerical, institutional, and hierarchical model that had prevailed; to affirm the dignity of the laity in the Church; to establish through a more conciliatory attitude, through some new theological insights, and through effective mechanism a better relationship with other religious bodies, looking ultimately to the healing of the divisions in Christianity and fruitful "dialogue" with non-Christian religions; to change the teaching of the Church on "religious liberty" and give new support to the principle of "freedom of conscience"; to base theology and biblical studies more firmly on historical principles; to foster styles of piety based more obviously on Scripture and the public liturgy of the Church; to affirm clearly that the Church was and should be affected by the cultures in which it exercises its ministries; finally, to promote a more positive appreciation of "the world" and the relationship of the Church to it, with a concomitant assumption of clearer responsibility for the fate of the world in "the new era" that the Council saw opening up before its eyes.

The very comprehensiveness of this listing, along with the *de facto* changes in attitude and practice it necessitated, suggests that we are dealing here with something more than a "reform." Moreover, disparate though the individual aims may seem to be when listed in such an abstract way, they do have a logical or affective relationship among themselves and originate from a new ecclesiological or theological paradigm. For one thing, many of these aims moderate or even reverse positions that crystallized in the Middle Ages and the Counter Reformation. In essence, however, the new paradigm wanted to effect a Church responsive to "the needs of the times." The paradigm bore within itself therefore, the basis for its program, which was identical with the content of the paradigm as it was actually elaborated by the Council.

Of all the changes in attitude that the Council seemed to permit or promote, few were more profound in their implications than that there was "salvation outside the Church," even outside Christianity. The Council is cautious here. But if we contrast its documents, especially those relating to persons or institutions outside the Roman Catholic Church, with the pronouncement of Pope Boniface VIII in 1302, we see what is at stake: "Furthermore, we declare, state, and define that it is absolutely necessary to salvation that every human creature be subject to the Roman Pontiff."[34] No matter how that pronouncement is interpreted, it indicates an attitude from which the Council sedulously distanced itself.[35] The position that the Council took on the issue reflects its new "world consciousness" and its recognition of the pluralism of the contemporary situation. More important still, it is symptomatic of the radical implications of the new paradigm; the repercussions that this position on "salvation outside the Church" has for Christology, soteriology, and ecclesiology are enormous and are only now beginning to be elaborated.[36]

In adjusting itself in this and other ways to a "world consciousness," the Council gave shape to its own paradigm of the Church. After recourse to its own tradition, the Council determined that the Church could and should in fact refashion its own paradigm to bring it more into accord with conditions

[34]Henricus Denzinger and Adolphus Schönmetzer, ed., *Enchiridion symbolorum* (33rd ed.; Rome: Herder, 1965) 281: "Porro subesse Romano Pontifici omni humanae creaturae declaramus, dicimus, diffinimus omnino esse de necessitate salutis."

[35]See, e.g., Rahner, "Interpretation of Vatican II" 720.

[36]See, e.g., J. Peter Schineller, "Christ and the Church: A Spectrum of Views," in *Why the Church?* ed. Walther J. Burghardt, S.J., and William G. Thompson, S.J. (New York: Paulist, 1977) 1-22; reprinted from *TS* 37 (1976) 545-66.

"out there." The need of the Church at present, a need legiti-
mated by the tradition itself, was to accommodate to the present situation.

We thus arrive at the authenticity test for the formal and
material aspects of the Council's paradigm. On what basis
were the many changes it promoted justified? The ultimate
justification was the self-validating authority of the Council
itself, but the more immediate one was, in fact, the "needs of
the times." The test was coterminous with the paradigm.

When the test is compared with the ones adduced in the
Gregorian and Lutheran reformations, it lacks the more focused and specific quality that those enjoyed. The lack of
focus here points to the lack of a single "focused issue," in
contrast with those reformations. Nothing is more characteristic of Vatican II than the breadth of its concerns, never
neatly packaged into a central issue.

Moreover, the needs of the times are so variously perceived
in the concrete by different individuals and groups that their
probative force as an authenticity test is infinitely more dis-
sipated than an appeal to the sacred canons or to the Epistle to
the Romans. Which needs? Whose needs? To what realities
and to what extent may the test legitimately be applied by a
Church that wholeheartedly believes in the divine origin of its
constitution? Herein lies a fundamental problem in the "structure of the content" of Vatican II that is quite different from
the analogous problem in the two reformations.

The Rhetoric of Vatican II

Despite these and other ambiguities and even ambivalences,
the Council certainly provoked a crisis within Roman Catholicism—a fact that I assume does not need proof or detailed
description here. That crisis did not manifest itself in such a
dramatic way as did Gregory's conflict with the Emperor or
the religious wars that followed upon the Protestant Reformation. This fact could be interpreted as a sign that the crisis
was not so deep as those provoked in the other two instances,
but crisis it was, in any case.

Part of the reason for the less dramatic nature of the crisis surely rests with the style of rhetoric the Council adopted in presenting itself to the world and the Church. It conciliated and reassured rather than confronted. This time the slogan was *aggiornamento*, updating. In a culture used to the attempts of almost every institution to "modernize" and "streamline" itself from time to time, this slogan could be counted upon to appeal to many. It could function as cheer, even loyalty test, but hardly as battle cry—at least not a battle cry from those directly responsible for the decisions of the Council, the bishops. *Aggiornamento* exemplifies the conciliatory or "soft" rhetoric that the Council consistently employed. It was litotes, a rhetorical understatement.[37] Its equivalents like "renewal" and "renovation" substituted for terms like "reformation" that, because of their historical connotations, were far more threatening.[38]

These considerations begin to indicate how widely the Council's rhetoric differed from the denunciatory stance assumed by both Gregory and Luther. The documents of the Council were deliberately structured in a discursive, even homiletical, way— quite different from the apodictic style of Gregory and Luther, and different even from the condemnatory canons that have traditionally been the literary forms councils employed in their decrees. Indeed, the "rhetoric of reproach" is almost wholly absent from the Council, at least as applied to identifiable persons, groups, ideas, or movements. There are no palpable and clear enemies. The "rhetoric of reproach" is replaced by a "rhetoric of congratulation." This stance may well be religiously admirable, but it is rhetorically problematic; for it induces a vagueness and indeterminacy into language that deprives it of dramatic force.

On the other hand, the Council certainly engaged in a

---

[37]See Philippe Levillain, *La méchanique politique de Vatican II: La majorité et l'unanimité dans un concile* (Paris: Beauchesne, 1975) 35-36: "Il [*aggiornamento*] représentait une litote subtile entre les deux termes inexprimables de 'Réforme' et d' 'Autocritique,' traçait à l'Église une perspective de réflexion sur elle-même et proposait un Concile qui n'était dirigé contre personne parce qu'il l'était en réalité 'contre' l'Église elle-même, pour dégager le neuf du permanent et vivifier son éternité."

[38]See my "Reform, Historical Consciousness" above, pp. 62-63.

"rhetoric of great expectations" in many of its documents. Both implicitly and explicitly it held out, for instance, promise of a world of religious harmony in which competing churches and religious traditions would somehow be brought together. Especially in *Gaudium et spes*, it held out hopes for a world in which justice and peace would reign and in which religion and technology would co-operate for a more humane environment. The optimism of this document has often been noted. It helped create a vision of hope in a world receptive to such a message. But visions of hope, unless somehow soon realized, tend after a short while to be forgotten or to turn sour. It seems to be true, unfortunately, that the "rhetoric of reproach" has more staying power.[39]

The refusal by the Council to engage in vituperation extended to the practices and attitudes that it was in fact repudiating. The Council heads off in a new direction often without indication than an older direction has been abandoned, without much indication even of what that older direction was. In other words, explicit redefinition of what was good and bad—vernacular liturgy rather than Latin liturgy, conciliatory rather than polemical attitudes towards the churches of the Reformation, and similar matters—had to be done by "experts" outside the Council. These experts quite often indulged in sharp criticism of the preconciliar situation. In lectures, in books, in articles in both popular and learned journals, and in jokes at cocktail parties, deficiencies and aberrations were pointed out. This activity took place, however, apart from the official texts of the Council. Today, twenty years after the Council, its conciliatory language produces notable problems for anyone trying to teach its documents to a generation born after the Council closed.

An even more confusing situation occurs at those points in the documents of the Council where the "new" is simply placed alongside the "old", with the apparent assumption that they

---

[39]See Quintilian, *Institutiones oratoriae* 3, 8, 40: "For quite apart from the fact that the minds of unprincipled men are easily swayed by terror, I am not sure that most men's minds are not more easily influenced by fear of evil than by hope of good, for they find it easier to understand what is evil than what is good" (Loeb tr.).

are mutually compatible and both equally valid. The now classic example of this problem, of course, is how to relate chapter 3 in *Lumen gentium*, which treats the hierarchical character of the Church, to the rest of the document. The vertical "hierarchical Church" and the more horizontal "people-of-God Church" may be reconcilable, but the documents do not clearly tell us how to effect that reconciliation. Such unclarity even permits the disturbing question to arise in some people's minds not of what new direction or paradigm it was that the Council advocated but whether in fact there was a new direction or paradigm advocated at all. It is necessary to *argue*, as I have been doing, that there was indeed such a new direction or paradigm.

In contrast, therefore, with the rhetoric of the Gregorian and Lutheran reformations, the rhetoric of the Council lacks sharpness and clarity. The interpretation of its documents is even more susceptible of manipulation than most other reform documents in the history of the Christian Church, especially as we move away from the event itself.[40] However much distaste we might feel for the vituperative language in which both Gregory and Luther indulged, that language supplied clear indication of what was right and what was wrong, of what was to be embraced and of what was to be repudiated—embraced and repudiated, moreover, with all one's heart and with all one's strength, at the risk of one's life.

Nonetheless, the Council evoked a crisis in Catholicism. How is this fact to be explained? In a Church that by and large distinguished itself from other Christian bodies in the West by its confession of unbroken continuity with its venerable past, the slogan of *aggiornamento*, for all its surface appeal, had bite. Attempts to downplay its innovative character, moreover, had to face the reality of the adjustments in practice and attitude with which it consistently confronted the faithful. Never before in the history of Catholicism had so many changes been legislated and implemented that immediately touched the lives of common folk, and never before had such

---

[40]See Acerbi, "Receiving Vatican II."

radical adjustments of viewpoint been so abruptly required of them. The verbal rhetoric of the Council may have been reassuring; the "rhetoric of action" that accompanied it was not.

The changes the Council mandated were thrust upon a membership that was psychologically and theologically unprepared to receive them. Elements of the "new paradigm" that before the Council had been gestating in the minds of some theologians had never been allowed to mature even in academic circles in an atmosphere of healthy give and take, and the faithful had been kept even more carefully sheltered from any suggestion that certain issues were under discussion. The advantages of the Latin liturgy, for instance, had been deeply inculcated upon the minds and hearts of the faithful up to the time the Council opened. It is now easy to forget, moreover, the restrictions that John Courtney Murray suffered for his ideas on religious liberty.

When the changes came, they burst upon the scene. Some of them, like the changes in the liturgy, were implemented in autocratic fashion, with little or no attempt to explain them. The "rhetoric" of the Council, now viewed broadly to include the actions that interpreted the words, was more assertive, therefore, than it at first seems. Paradoxically, the conciliatory language of the Council was accompanied by an autocratic manner of implementing the decisions of the Council. In many ways the language did not correlate with the kinds of changes that began to take place. Crisis, or at least confusion, was the almost inevitable result.

Leadership

One of the greatest contrasts between the changes effected by Vatican II and those effected by the two reformations is that the former emanated from a committee, whereas the latter were causes assumed by two individuals utterly committed to visions they had made their own. By the time the Council was over, the participants did not lack enthusiasm for its *aggiornamento* but, due to the very matrix in which *aggiornamento* came into being, they did lack passion for it.

"Pope John's Council," as it finally turned out, could only remotely be claimed by him. The great pope deserves credit for convoking the Council, but there is not the slightest shred of evidence that he foresaw or intended the direction it took. In any case, he died early in the Council and, again by the very nature of the case that would have prevailed even if he had survived, his successors were only implementers of decisions taken by a group.

The unclarities, the hesitations, the qualifications, the ambivalences that mark the documents reflect the huge committee in which they were hammered out. They were the price paid to obtain consensus. They reflect the work of a committee, whose members went home to resume life pretty much as usual once the work was done. Gregory and Luther never "went home."

The very comprehensiveness of the documents and their care not to offend, as well as their concern to satisfy various constituencies, militated against their being assumed by any individual as passionately his own. It can be questioned, in fact, just how clearly some of the fathers understood what they had wrought and now had to communicate to constituencies that understood less than they did.

All this is not to underestimate what that "huge committee" accomplished. I know of no other such assembly in history that undertook such a bold reshaping of the institution it represented, and did it with more fairness, serenity, and courage. The care to win, not impose, consensus was a hallmark of the Council, as exemplified by its insistence on at least a two-thirds majority, soon leading almost to unanimity, for all its important steps.[41] Nonetheless, the problems inherent in such assemblies and in the "committee documents" they produce must not be underestimated. As some of the leading figures at the Council such as Cardinals Bea, Lercaro, and Suenens pass from the scene, the problem of leadership becomes more crucial than ever.

To Paul VI fell the task, in the first instance, of carrying forward the decisions and spirit of the Council once it closed.

---

[41]The most thorough analysis of this aspect of the Council is Levillain, *La méchanique politique.*

The criticisms he had to suffer from both "right" and "left" suggest how difficult the task was, how unclear the mandate. The fact that the next two pontiffs deliberately made the names of the two conciliar popes their own—John and Paul—indicates the recognized obligation of further implementation. The anomaly of the problem of leadership for the Council appears here in symbolic form: the chief implementer of a Council that opted in favor of a less centralized and less hierarchical polity turns out to be, in most people's minds, the central authority of the Church, the top figure in the hierarchical pyramid.

Institutional Grounding

In my opinion, the ultimate key to success of the two reformations lay neither in the content nor the rhetoric nor the leadership that characterized them, but in their eventual grounding in new or ongoing institutions. They both created, for instance, a new social class that had high stakes in the success of the reformation. They thus wove themselves into the fabric of society in ways that made it virtually impossible to reverse course without destroying the class.

The Second Vatican Council was cautious regarding the structures within the Church. Few, if any, institutions were obliterated. Even the Holy Office, so severely criticized and ridiculed during the Council, escaped with a reorganization and a new name; it was not abolished. Episcopal Conferences, already a reality in the Church, received conciliar codification and blessing, and the Synod of Bishops was inaugurated. Both these institutions were meant to give palpable substance to a theology of episcopal collegiality.

Many people pinned great hopes on the Conferences and on the Synod. Only time will tell how great the impact of these two institutions will be. On certain issues the National Conference of Bishops in the United States, for instance, has demonstrated a capacity for courageous leadership. Institutions have a curious way of assuming a life of their own and playing a role unforeseen by their creators and members. Sometimes that role does not emerge until decades or centuries after their founding. Nonetheless, these two institutions lack clear definition of their powers, and their decision-making processes up to now seem to be more *sub Petro* than *cum Petro*. Neither the Conferences nor the Synod represents, in any case, the investing of a new class with high stakes in *aggiornamento*. They are, therefore, quite different from the institutions that came into being in the two reformations.

The closest historical parallel to the Synod and Conferences I can think of is the institution resulting from the decree *Frequens* of the Council of Constance in 1417. According to that solemn and never officially repudiated decree of perhaps the most important of all the medieval councils, the pope was bound to convoke a council henceforth in perpetuity at clearly stated intervals. The provisions of the decree were duly observed by Pope Martin V when he convoked the Council of Pavia-Siena, 1423, and the Council of Basel, 1431. But after the severe crisis occasioned by the latter, the decree became a dead letter. It had created, you will note, no new social class whose very existence depended on its implementation.

Sometimes, of course, new classes come into being by default or indirection. Luther did not calculate that he was creating a new class when he advocated clerical marriage, but he made a decision that eventuated in a new class. Perhaps something along that line is happening today, not because of any specific decision Vatican II took along this line, but because of the impact the Council had among Catholics on their general appreciation of the Church, its ministry, and the role of the laity in the Church.

One of the most striking, even alarming, phenomena in postconciliar Catholicism has been the dramatic decline in priestly and religious vocations in many parts of the world. This decline has been taken as one of the signs of "the postconciliar crisis." The decline may be only temporary but the indications are not reassuring. The slack is being taken up, however, and the traditional ministries of the Church are being exercised now increasingly in certain parts of the world by lay volunteers and lay professionals—men and women, single and married.

The laity has a different education, a different experience of life, and a different incorporation into church and society than does the clergy as we know it today. Its psychological and religious profile cannot at present be charted, but it is surely different in many respects from that of the official clergy. Although not identified with the program of the Council, lay ministry is an indirect result of it and finds its theological justification in the Council's affirmation of the priesthood of all believers.[42]

"Class" is a vague word, and it becomes vaguer when applied to a phenomenon like this one. Furthermore, one can hardly state that this new class of ministers has a life-and-death stake in the shape of *aggiornamento*. Moreover, lay ministry is not as totally new in the Church as we sometimes believe; religious sisters and brothers, for instance, have long engaged in activities that can be described as ministry. The difference today is that the laity is doing things once reserved exclusively to priests. In that sense it is a new reality in Catholicism, and its implications for the future are altogether unpredictable.[43] The apprehensions in certain circles today regarding the whole question of ministry indicates that a sensitive nerve is being touched. The present "crisis in ministry" is part of the legacy of the Council, and it may indicate that through it a new institutional grounding is taking place.

From the very moment that Pope John XXIII announced on January 25, 1959, that he intended to convoke a council, the most obvious and explicit instrument for its institutional grounding was to be the revision of the Code of Canon Law. Now that the new Code is completed and promulgated, scholars are examining it to see how faithfully it reflects the Council and carries it forward. Some are disappointed with its

---

[42]See *Apostolicam actuositatem* 10 (AAS 58 [1966] 846).

[43]See, e.g., the report by the U.S. Bishops' National Advisory Council, "The Thrust of Lay Ministry," *Origins* 9 (1980) 621-26, and the reflections of the bishops of the United States, "Called and Gifted: Catholic Laity 1980," ibid 10 (1980) 369-73. The latter document states: "Ecclesial ministers, i.e., lay persons who have prepared for professional ministry in the Church, represent a new development. We welcome this as a gift to the church" (372).

caution; others believe it is an appropriate, probably only provisional, step forward.[44]

In some of its provisions the new Code surely reflects the theology of the laity found in key documents of the Council. The Code provides, for instance, for mandatory involvement of the laity in all financial matters pertaining to diocesan and parochial life; the laity may perform all the functions of an ordained deacon when particular conditions so warrant; the removal of the old canon that limited a pastor to one parish opens the way for laity and members of the "consecrated life" (religious) to perform the day-to-day care of souls previously reserved to priests. Thus the new Code, while reaffirming the traditional Roman-law theories 'of polity, also admits a pastoral practice and theology that in certain ways runs counter to an older structure. The suggestions of a grounding of a paradigmatic shift seem to be present.[45]

Conclusion

By now it is clear that, although the *aggiornamento* of Vatican II in some ways resembles the two reformations I have delineated, it also differs from them considerably. The Council most clearly resembles the Gregorian and Lutheran reformations in that it constructed a new paradigm of religious consciousness and Church order, a paradigm that departed in significant ways from the one in possession before the Council began. In the documents of the Council this paradigm generally displaces the older one, while on a few occasions it coexists uneasily alongside it. With the construction of a new paradigm, a series of redefinitions concomitantly took place. These redefinitions were usually only implicit and were thus characteristic of the essentially conciliatory rhetoric of the Council, in contrast with the more denunciatory and assertive rhetoric of both Gregory and Luther. A more assertive and

---

[44]See Abelli, "Ein Grundgesetz."

[45]See, e.g., Francis Morrisey, "The Laity and the Threefold Mission of the Church," *Canon Law Society Great Britain and Ireland Newsletter* 25 (1982) 130-55. See also Winfried Aymans, "Ecclesiological Implications of the New Legislation," ibid. 38-73. I am indebted to John T. Finnegan, adjunct professor of canon law, Weston School of Theology, for these references and for a number of suggestions concerning this article.

confronting element was present, however, in the manner in which some of the decisions of the Council were implemented. The leadership exercised by the Council and Council's institutional grounding appear at present notably weaker than in either the Gregorian or Lutheran reformations, but it is too early to judge, especially for the institutional grounding. There is, therefore, no point-for-point correlation between Vatican II and either of these other two phenomena.

Where does this leave us in our assessment? First, we must recall that the Gregorian and Lutheran reformations are in no way prescriptive or normative for other self-induced changes on a large scale that might occur at some given time in the history of the Christian Church. These two reformations provide models for comparison and supply materials from which to construct some instruments of analysis; nothing more—or less. No historical event or phenomenon ever repeats itself. This is true of the two reformations. My analysis of them designedly highlighted their similarities, thereby doing violence to the immense differences that distinguish them from one another. There is no reason to anticipate that Vatican II would altogether tally even with the similarities I have indicated between these reformations. Indeed, we should a priori expect that the differences would far outweigh the likenesses.

The second consideration of absolutely fundamental importance, to which I have so far only casually called attention, is not the correlation between the two reformations themselves but between each of them and the culture in which they achieved their success. In ways almost too complex to analyze, each of them reflected and promoted developments in society at large that assured their success at least as much as the four factors I isolated for the sake of comparison between them. The centralizing tendencies of the Gregorians reflected and promoted similar tendencies in secular society as Western Europe began to emerge from the feudal age; as the "papal monarch" rose to prominence, so did national monarchies. We can not adequately speak about religious paradigms without locating them in the larger cultural context.

This consideration is not meant to minimize the aggressive energies of the reformations viewed in themselves, but to emphasize that they were not self-contained realities. Earlier I made the point that changes that take place "outside" the Church result in "developments" within the Church. It is, accordingly, also true that no "reformation" within the Church can ultimately succeed unless it correlates with some realities "out there." The reason is obvious: the same human person is both member of the Church and citizen of the world.

Whatever the intrinsic force of a reformation, it has to be "received" to be effective. Any movement that is too much at odds with general culture is bound to fail or remain marginal, unless, of course, it is carried forward by sheer violence. Only if the movement is somehow co-ordinate with the hopes, grievances, mentality, and structures of society at large does it have a chance of success. If the movement is thus co-ordinated, even imperfectly, the culture itself contains a momentum that after a certain point tends to carry the movement along, most probably in ways that transcend the intentions of the original creators.

Most characteristic of Vatican II was precisely its effort to co-ordinate itself with general culture. The very nature of this enterprise suggests why the rhetoric of the Council differed from the rhetoric of Gregory and Luther. The rhetoric differed because the enterprises were different. The Council adopted a conciliatory rhetoric because it was engaged in a conciliatory task.

Initially the Council meant to speak only to the Roman Catholic Church, but as it moved along it extended its message to "the whole of humanity." There were thus two sets of addressees: those within the Roman Catholic Church and all those outside it. Even when the Council spoke to Catholics, it was not only to put them in touch with the deeper roots of their own tradition but often to show them how that tradition could respond more effectively to conditions "outside." In so far as there was an element of confrontation in the rhetoric of the Council, it was directed for the most part to members of the Roman Catholic Church. The Council confronted those who could be presumed to agree with it; it conciliated those who on the surface seemed far removed from sympathy with what it represented. The complexity of the Council's undertaking manifests itself in the complexity, in almost the tangle, of its rhetoric. The rhetoric of the Council is thus intimately related to its enterprise. That enterprise was complex—but also unique and unprecedented in that a major change was undertaken not in prophetic opposition to something but as an act of profound reconciliation. If this was what was unique about the Council, then it is here we must especially look in order to assess it.

To assess Vatican II, therefore, we must return to the radical nature of *aggiornamento*. The material aspects of that principle as the Council actually formulated them are, of course, important. Far more important, it seems to me, is the formal aspect, i.e., the admission of the principle of deliberate reconciliation between the Church and certain changes taking place outside it.

This admission implies a continuation after the Council of the open-ended agenda that characterized the Council itself. If we are now "beyond" the Council, that is where we should be. Important though specific decisions were and continue to be, more important would be the continuing, and inevitable, dialogue of the Church with the world outside it. The central point of contact was the new historical consciousness that pervades modern culture and that had such impact on the Council itself. This consciousness meant an admission of contingency on a scale larger than was ever admitted before. By admitting the principle, the Council admitted the inevitability of ongoing change, admitted the impossibility of being immune to such change.

As I illustrated earlier, many of the most profound changes that have taken place in the history of the Church were not the result, in the first instance, of self-conscious initiative on the part of Church membership. There is no reason to believe that the situation is any different today, except perhaps more intensified because of the mass media and the fast pace of contemporary culture. Few cultural developments in the past hundred years are as important as the pervasive influence of the idea of historical contingency, and there is little reason to believe that this idea will not continue to influence theology and Church order.

In other words, unlike the Gregorian and the Lutheran

reformations, where the critical point for success seems to have been institutional grounding, the critical point for Vatican II may well be in the idea, in the paradigm. Whereas, in those reformations the paradigm flew in the face of convention, in this instance it represents a belated recognition of the already established reality of the new historical consciousness. There are other established realities to which it relates as well: the emergence of democracy as a favored political form, the world as global village, a new religious and cultural pluralism, and similar phenomena. The reality "out there," so ingrained into the way we think and judge, seems to be where the long-range grounding of the Council may lie. Thus, though it may be possible in particular instances and for a short while to resist or deny the paradigm, the reality of the new consciousness will persist and have its effects.

It is important to recall that many, even most, political revolutions have been followed by some attempt at "restoration." Restorations moderate excesses, but they do so by positing a dreamworld that artificially reconstructs the conditions of days gone by. The unreality of that world guarantees that it will not last long. The proponents of the Gregorian and the Lutheran reformations soon experienced disappointment at what seemed to be the futility of their efforts and the dissipation of their visions. But both of these movements were too much in concert with their epochs to go down in defeat. Forces outside them began, sometimes unwittingly and unwillingly, to carry them forward.

Was Vatican II, then, another "great reformation"? If it was, it was quite different from the other two. Nonetheless, despite the complexity of its rhetoric, despite the weakness of its leadership and institutional grounding, I am inclined to answer in the affirmative. There are, however, signs to the contrary.

Perhaps we would be on less contested, and more helpful, ground if we simply rephrased the question. Was Vatican II at least symptomatic of a huge change in perception and in ways of thinking, judging, and acting that mark modern culture and that therefore will inevitably continue to mark the course of theology and Church order? Here the answer can be a sturdier affirmative. By this affirmative we assess both Vatican II and the general situation of the Church and ourselves in contemporary culture—which was the point of the question about Vatican II in the first place. There is little doubt in my mind that the Roman Catholic Church has in the past twenty years entered a new era of its history. The Council is more responsible than any other single agent for the formal inception of that era.

No large institution will overnight transform its paradigm into something entirely different; no institution ever continues over a long period of time to operate wholly on the same paradigm, especially not an institution so deeply imbedded in human culture as the Roman Catholic Church. The persistent Catholic impulse to reconcile "nature and grace" is, when raised to the level of social institutions, an impulse to reconcile the Church with human culture in all its positive dimensions—with sin excepted and the gospel affirmed. In that sense the Council, for all its daring, moved solidly in line with the Catholic tradition. The Church is fully incorporated into human history, and changes that take place there deeply affect it. That is what the Council saw, and that perception is perhaps its best legacy. That is what it means to belong to a Church that, as the Council insisted, is truly a pilgrim in this world. That is the continuing challenge of the Council to us all.

6

Priesthood, Ministry, and Religious Life: Some Historical and Historiographical Considerations

This article has a simple thesis: the categories with which we customarily think about religious life are inadequate to the historical reality and that inadequacy is to a large extent responsible for some of the confusion in the Church today about religious life, especially about the relationship to priesthood and ministry of the "regular clergy," i.e., priests living in a religious order or congregation under a rule. This confusion, I further maintain, is harmful to religious orders and congregations, even those that do not have ordained members, and is also harmful in the long run to the Church as a whole.

The confusion has roots deep in our past, but it remained latent or at least virtually unnamed until quite recently. Forcing it ever more into our awareness have been the implications and implementation of certain documents of Vatican Council II, especially *Presbyterorum ordinis* on the "ministry and life of priests." *Optatam totius* on the "training of priests," *Christus Dominus* on the "pastoral office of bishops," and *Perfectae caritatis* on "the renewal of religious life." An altogether crucial question has emerged: How do religious priests fit in the ministry of the Church?

If we turn to the Council, we do not find an altogether satisfactory answer, although we are left free to infer that the specific difference between religious and diocesan priests lies in the fact that the former take vows of poverty, chastity, and obedience, whereas the latter do not. The ideals that these vows entail, however, are so vigorously enjoined upon diocesan priests themselves in *Presbyterorum ordinis* that in the long run the difference seems to be at most one of emphasis or consists simply in the juridical fact of public vows, or perhaps life in community.[1] The difference seems thus reducible to some rather subtle particularities of spirituality which in fact are almost impossible to define. The conclusion that seems to follow is that there is one priesthood,[2] but priests can be animated by different spiritualities.[3] There are no further differences. Although *Presbyterorum ordinis* concedes that its provisions are to be applied to regular clergy only insofar as they "suit their circumstances," the document seems to assume that they in fact "suit their circumstances" quite well.[4] The topic sentence of the opening paragraph sets the tone for everything that follows: "What is said here applies to all priests."[5]

Some things surely do apply to all. The Council, for instance, locates priestly identity to a large extent in ministry, a location surely pertinent to both diocesan and religious clergy.[6] Yet it is with this very issue of ministry that the problem begins to manifest itself. The basic design in *Presbyterorum ordinis* for priestly ministry, implicit though it is, has three essential components: it is a ministry by and large to the faithful; it is a ministry conceived as taking place in a stable community of faith; it is a ministry done by clergy in "hier-

---

[1] Nos. 15-17.

[2] See ibid., no. 7.

[3] See *Christus Dominus* (henceforth *CD*), no. 33.

[4] *Presbyterorum ordinis* (henceforth *PO*), no. 1. Unless otherwise noted, English translations are from *Documents of Vatican II*, ed. Austin P. Flannery (Grand Rapids: Eerdmans, 1975).

[5] Ibid.

[6] On the unresolved conflict in *PO* between the "classic" theology of priesthood and a "poco tradizionale" presentation of ministry, see Christian Duquoc, "La riforma dei chierici," in *Il Vaticano II e la chiesa*, ed. Giuseppe Alberigo and Jean-Pierre Jossua (Brescia: Paideia, 1985) 399-414.

archical union with the order of bishops."[7]

This design corresponds to the ministerial traditions and situation of the diocesan clergy. But does it correspond to the traditions and situation of the religious clergy? Not so clearly. In fact, it practically contradicts them—as I hope to make clear in this article, if it is not clear already. Moreover, we must note that the Council ties ministry to questions of church order when it speaks so repeatedly and insistently of "hier-archical union with the order of bishops." Yet, the major religious orders and congregations have lived in a tradition of exemption from episcopal jurisdiction, to a large extent even for their ministry. If we are to understand the sense of dis-location in some religious at the present time, I therefore con-tend, we must direct our attention not so much to issues of spirituality, in the conventional sense of the term, but to issues of ministry and church order.

As a background to Vatican II, I will review these two issues in the history of religious life from about the 13th to the late-16th centuries, when traditions that affected the modern Church were set. I deal explicitly with clerical orders and con-gregations of men, for it is only with them that the question of ordained priesthood arises. Ministry is, however, an issue also for most orders and congregations of women and for non-clerical congregations of men. It is an issue for the laity. For lack of space and competence, I do not address these aspects of the problem, but I assume that where my observations and conclusions might apply to these women and men will be clear. For the same reasons I have had to restrict myself almost exclusively to the Dominicans, Franciscans, and Jesuits, but I believe that what I say applies *mutatis mutandis* to others.

Some Historiographical Traditions

We cannot examine "what happened" until we examine the categories in which we frame what happened. We must there-

---

[7]*PO*, no. 7. The idea recurs, e.g., ibid, nos. 2, 4, 5, 6, 8, 12; *CD*, nos. 28, 34; *Optatam totius* (henceforth *OT*), no. 2.

fore examine certain historiographical traditions. I am convinced that the origin of part of our confusion about priesthood and ministry in religious orders and congregations lies in some inadequate but popular and widely appropriated historical grids. That is to say, whether we realize it or not, we think about these issues in historical frameworks that we do not question.

The historiography of any phenomenon falls into patterns that form at certain moments and then tend to persist for decades, generations, or even longer. This is especially true for standard and general histories, for it takes a long time for monographic studies to challenge the received wisdom that such texts tend to repeat without re-examination. Moreover, the historiography of any given phenomenon tends to take on a life of its own, isolated from the historiography of even related phenomena, so that integration of the results of research from different areas or disciplines is a slow and usually imperfect process.

We are in fact dealing in this article with the history of five imperfectly distinct phenomena: (1) ministry and priesthood, (2) church order, (3) religious life, (4) spirituality, (5) church reform. Although in some of their basic premises the historiographical traditions of these phenomena are quite valid, they suffer from certain defects along the lines I indicated above, which in many instances can be reduced to the fallacy of misplaced emphasis. At this point I want simply to describe the patterns, in as brief and clear a manner as possible, and to suggest how they might need to be modified. My critique goes somewhat as follows.

1. Histories of priesthood and ministry, as we now have them, deal almost exclusively with data from the biblical and patristic periods, to the almost complete neglect of the traditions of the Church during the Middle Ages through the modern period up to Vatican II.[8] That neglect of some 1500

---

[8]Typical of this tendency is the otherwise excellent survey by Nathan Mitchell, *Mission and Ministry: History and Theology in the Sacrament of Order* (Wilmington, Del.: Glazier, 1982). See also Edward Schillebeeckx, *Ministry: Leadership in the Community of Jesus Christ* (New York: Crossroad, 1981); Joseph Lécuyer, *Le*

years, I propose, give us a curiously unbalanced and incomplete picture of our traditions of these important institutions. 2. The scant attention that these histories sometimes concede to that long period consists almost exclusively in *ideas* about priesthood or sacred orders that Aquinas or the Council of Trent, for instance, proffered. They thus do not deal with what was actually *happening* in ministry, in church order, in culture at large, and therefore, for this portion of their presentation, woefully brief, they fall into simply a history of ideas. I propose that what Aquinas and Trent *said* about ministry and priesthood did not necessarily correspond to the *experience* of ministry and priesthood even for their own times. What we desperately lack at present is a comprehensive study of the history of ministerial *practice* from the 12th to the 20th centuries, although we are now beginning to possess the monographic studies in *social* history that would make such a synthesis possible.[9]

3. Whereas histories of ministry do sometimes deal with institutions as well as ideas when they discuss the biblical and patristic periods (though not subsequent periods) general histories of spirituality for all periods have fallen almost exclusively into the pattern of the history of ideas. Their concern is what saints and spiritual authors *thought* about prayer, mortification, spiritual reading, the sacraments, and even religious experience itself. Generally missing, therefore, is any indication

---

sacrement de l'ordination (Paris: Beauchesne, 1983); Albert Vanhoye, *Old Testament Priests and the New Priest according to the New Testament* (Petersham, Mass.: St. Bede's, 1986). In his second book on ministry, Schillebeeckx' treatment of our period is still brief, but especially perceptive and helpful: *The Church with the Human Face: A New and Expanded Theology of Ministry* (New York: Crossroad, 1985). The only book of which I am aware that attempts a chronologically evenhanded treatment is Bernard Cooke, *Ministry to Word and Sacrament: History and Theology* (Philadelphia: Fortress, 1976). Commendable though this book is in so many ways, it approaches these centuries with a somewhat different perspective than myself and without utilizing the same information.

[9] The current tidal wave of social history has made practically no impact here. See e.g., B.-D. Marliangeas, *Clés pour une théologie du ministère* (Paris: Beauchesne, 1978). For some issues connected with social history and for bibliography, see Peter Burke, "Popular Religion," forthcoming in *Catholicism in Early Modern History: A Guide to Research*, ed. John W. O'Malley (St Louis: Center for Reformation Research, 1988).

of how these devout persons might fill up a day or, more important, how they engaged in ministry, what instruments they might have devised for ministry.[10]

4. The title of David Knowles' little classic on the history of religious life, *From Pachomius to Ignatius*, clearly indicates the pattern with which we habitually frame this complex phenomenon.[11] We see religious life as a continuous development, out of the cenobitic traditions, of the search for personal perfection. The matrix for the development is thus decidedly monastic. True, there was an "active" element in monasticism almost from the beginning. True, as time moved forward some monasteries and other institutions enriched the tradition by being even more "active" in the world. But, I ask, do not the "active orders" constitute more of a break with the tradition than the from-Pachomius-to-Ignatius pattern superficially suggests? If those orders are viewed not as the institutional embodiment of an ascetical tradition traced back to Pachomius, but as a critically important phenomenon in the history of ministry claiming "apostolic" inspiration, different appreciations and new issues emerge. In other words, at least from the 13th century, the history of religious orders pertains as much to the history of ministry as it does to the history of institutional asceticism.

5. The history of the religious orders, especially when incorporated into larger histories, is often seen as pertaining to the history of church reform. This is most obviously verified in the foundations of the Counter Reformation like the Jesuits and the Capuchins, but it is no less true for foundations in other periods. Most histories that deal with church reform tend to treat it in moralistic-disciplinary terms and, to a much lesser extent, in terms of doctrine. The religious orders are seen,

---

[10]See, e.g., the survey of literature by Massimo Marcocchi, "Spirituality," in *Catholicism*. See also, however, my "Introduction" to the so-called *spiritualia* of Erasmus, to be published in Vol. 66 of the *Collected Works of Erasmus* (Toronto: Univ of Toronto, 1988).

[11]Oxford: Clarendon Press, 1966. See now also Philip Rousseau, *Pachomius: The Making of a Community in Fourth-Century Egypt* (Berkeley: Univ of California, 1985).

therefore, usually in the context of their spiritualities, as "reforming morals and confirming doctrine," which is how the Council of Trent described its own task.[12] This historiographical tradition, which absolutely dominates the way most Catholics think about reform, ignores the important shifts in culture, ministry, church order, religious rhetoric, and propaganda that almost invariably accompany any reform and that in the long run are probably more important than any "moral reform" or "doctrinal confirmation" that might have taken place.

6. This situation is to a large extent the result of the tendency in the West to view church history from the perspective of a universalist ecclesiology. As Giuseppe Alberigo has recently observed, "The efforts made to elaborate a history of the Church 'from the base' or focused on popular religiosity remain largely inadequate and are still far from giving a satisfactory vision of the development, spatial and temporal, of the Christian experience as a communion of local communities."[13] Thus the various ways that ministry was effective or ineffective, especially in the long run, remain unstudied, or at least unincorporated into general presentations.

7. Although rarely recognized in standard histories, every reform program rests upon ecclesiological constructs like "the true Church," "the apostolic Church," "the evangelical Church," the well-disciplined Church," the "herald Church," the "sacramental Church."[14] There is an ecclesiology under every reform, and every ecclesiology relates directly to assumptions about ministry and church order. These ecclesiological constructs need to be exposed.

8. General histories that deal with church reform tend to

---

[12]See, e.g., the treatment of the mendicants and of the Jesuits in *Handbook of Church History,* ed. Hubert Jedin and John Dolan, 4 (Montreal: Palm, 1970) 172-83; 5 (New York: Seabury, 1980) 446-55.

[13]"The Local Church in the West (1500-1945)," *Heythrop Journal* 28 (1987) 125-43.

[14]I have shown this in great detail for one figure in *Giles of Viterbo on Church and Reform* (Leiden: Brill, 1968). See also, e.g., Gerhart B. Ladner, "Two Gregorian Letters: On the Sources and Nature of Gregory VII's Reform Ideology," *Studi Gregoriani* 5, (1956) 221-42.

rely too heavily upon official documents, like the decrees of Trent, and upon the *ideals* expressed by reformers, thereby neglecting what was actually happening "in the field."[15] Such histories need to be counterbalanced with *social* histories, which are concerned not with what people wanted to happen but with whether and how anything did happen and with its impact on the institutions of society.

9. Moreover, historians often fail to realize that the official documents of religious orders, including the documents of the founders themselves, express even the ideal only imperfectly. In particular, those documents find it easier to articulate how they are in continuity with the tradition than how they are innovating within it, for by the very nature of the case the latter reality lacks as yet a precise vocabulary. Those same documents are also incapable of rising above the historical realities in which they are immersed.[16] Only with the hindsight of generations or centuries does the *sensus plenior,* the full implication, emerge.

10. Finally, a general tendency in the historiography of all these phenomena must be mentioned: a tendency to read the past as a history of progress. Religious life, church reform, ministry, and similar institutions in this view thus move almost inexorably towards the balanced, comprehensive, and presumably definitive settlements of the contemporary Church, especially as expressed in the documents of Vatican II. One of the consequences of the subtle (and flattering) prejudice towards the present that underlies this tendency is that it admits no regress to a previous situation or condition. Paradoxically, it also does not admit much possibility of progress beyond the present. According to this style of thinking, the reforms of Vatican II, for instance, become definitive culminations of historical development, now frozen in their perfection, and

[15]See, e.g., a standard text like Justo L. González, *The Story of Christianity* 2 (San Francisco: Harper and Row, 1984) 14-121.

[16]See, e.g., my "The Fourth Vow in Its Ignatian Context: A Historical Study," *Studies in the Spirituality of Jesuits* 15, no. 1 (St. Louis: Seminar on Jesuit Spirituality, 1983), and "To Travel to Any Part of the World: Jerónimo Nadal and the Jesuit Vocation," ibid. 16, no. 2 (1984).

they do not of themselves invite us to further reflection and action in relationship to a reality that, by definition, can never achieve perfect expression in this world and that therefore requires constant readjustment.

Towards a Crucial Turning Point

What I now intend is to provide some historical evidence to support and illustrate the foregoing generalizations and show in more detail their implications. I will deal with just a few crucial moments in the period from the 13th century to the present. I am painfully aware that to accomplish adequately the task I have set myself would require several volumes dense with documentation, but for the moment I have to settle for nothing more than an interpretative essay, with all the perils inherent in such an enterprise.

I must assume that the reader is already familiar with some well-established findings about ministry, church order, and religious life from the period of the New Testament into the Middle Ages. These findings are extremely important for our purposes, but limitations of space indicate that nothing more than the briefest of summaries can be provided here.

The New Testament does not yield an altogether clear or consistent picture about church order, about the relationship between authority and community. Itinerant preaching is the pattern for ministry that emerges most obviously from these same documents, but different origins of missioning and commissioning for that ministry seem operative. Evidence for patterns of church order well into the second century is scarce, but eventually the now familiar pattern of a bishop surrounded by his presbyters emerged. From this point forward most of what we know about ministry during the patristic period derives from this now stable situation, in which the bishop and his clergy assume ever more fully certain traits of the Roman civil servant; the episcopacy becomes an *officium*, and the presbyter a *sacerdos*. Meanwhile, by the fifth century monastic and quasi-monastic communities have developed, and some

few of these engage in ministry in collaboration with the bishop.[17]
With the breakdown of public order in the early Middle Ages, some members of monastic communities began to take an ever-larger role in ministry. By now often without any relationship to the episcopacy, they became the great agents of evangelization until the tenth century. By the end of that century, however, "ministry," whether done by monks or "local" clergy, consisted to a large extent in various rituals and blessings and in the celebration of the liturgy. Evangelization, catechetics, and other traditional forms had practically disappeared in any organized form, and even preaching was considerably curtailed.[18]

With the 11th century a series of immensely important changes began to take place in society, as trade, cities, law, literacy, kingship, and other institutions took on new vitality. A great turning point had been reached and "the making of Europe" had begun. The Church was so integrally present to these phenomena that it can hardly be distinguished from them. For our purposes, however, two manifestations of change are particularly important.

The first is a phenomenon that took place at the upper level of European society, the so-called Investiture Controversy or Gregorian Reform, whose most dramatic expression was the battle unto death between Pope Gregory VII and Emperor Henry IV. The ramifications of that Reform for the internal life of the Church were incalculably great and are still being felt today. The most obviously direct of these ramifications was the emergence of a strong and centralized papacy and the concomitant emergence of a stronger episcopacy. The latter

[17]On these developments see, e.g., Mitchell, *Mission and Ministry*; Schillebeeckx, *Ministry*; Gerd Theissen, *Society of Early Palestinian Christianity* (Philadelphia: Fortress, 1978), and his *The Social Setting of Pauline Christianity* (Philadelphia: Fortress, 1982); Wayne Meeks, *The First Urban Christians: The Social World of the Apostle Paul* (New Haven: Yale Univ., 1983); Raymond E. Brown, *The Churches the Apostles Left Behind* (New York: Paulist, 1984); Adolar Zumkeller, *Das Mönchtum des heiligen Augustinus (Würzburg: Augustinus, 1950).*

[18]See, e.g., *Handbook of Church History* 3, 307-12, with bibliography.

was a result both of the Gregorian insistence on the ideal of episcopal independence from lay magnates and of the growth of cities, over which bishops presided. The revival of canon law that the Gregorians promoted gave support to an ideal of the bishop that emphasized his status in the hierarchical society of the times and vindicated his authority over certain properties and processes as over against his lay rival, the local nobility. The bishops' relationship to ministry as such was for a number of reasons not much considered in any direct fashion. In any case, the feudal age when abbots ruled the Church from their rural monasteries had begun to fade, as this important shift in church order took place.

The second phenomenon did not occur on the level of bishops and popes, but on a lower level of society. It included some clergy and monks, but also lay elites and rabble, and was in many ways more spontaneous that its Gregorian counterpart. Although it took a number of forms, it was unified by an enthusiasm for the "apostolic life," *vita apostolica* or *vita evangelica*.[19] With differing emphases that ideal included itinerant preaching, disdain for material goods, shunning and often denouncing the honors and social position that both Church and society offered. Increased literacy seems to have contributed somewhat to this ideal, for the "apostolic life" was vindicated on the basis of the way the "apostles" were presented in the New Testament. The "apostolic life" sought to recover the "apostolic Church."

This complex phenomenon was surely to some extent a "protest movement," reacting against the ostentatious wealth and status, especially of some of the upper clergy, that the new economic, social, and ecclesiastical conditions had already begun to produce. In some localities the enthusiasm for the "apostolic life" eventually turned sour. By the late-12th century, heretical movements like the Waldensians and the Albigensians— resulting from a strange mixture of learning and ignorance, of

---

[19]See, e.g., M.-H Vicaire, *L'Imitation des apôtres (Paris: Cerf, 1963).*

high ideals and smoldering resentments—became a wide-spread and public problem.[20]

The Dominicans and Franciscans

As we know so well, one "answer" to these heresies was the Dominican and Franciscan orders, both founded in the early 13th century.[21] They "answered" effectively because they were themselves part of the same enthusiasm for the *vita apostolica*, which included certain assumptions about ministry. We must look carefully, therefore, at the ministry of the friars. One of its most notable features was its origin. The ministry of the Dominicans clearly derived from a special and specific need, from a circumstance that fell outside the capabilities of the pastoral structures that were normatively in place. Those structures were impotent to deal with the Albigensians. For this period of church history, we can only with reservation describe those structures as "parochial," because parishes were not at this point the sociological reality they would eventually become.[22] But we can say that the structures were those under the local clergy that looked to the "normal" sacramental practice of the faithful. The Albigensians were, however, a radically alienated group, heretics, who scorned that practice and contemned the life-style of its ministers. Out of this situation was born the aptly named Order of Preachers.

[20]See, e.g., Tadeusz Manteufel, *Naissance d'une hérésie: Les adeptes de la pauvreté volontaire au Moyen Âge* (Paris: Mouton, 1970), and Handbook of Church History 3, 453-65; 4, 98-109, with bibliography.

[21]See, e.g., William A. Hinnebusch, *The History of the Dominican Order* (2 Vols. New York: Alba, 1965-73); M.-H. Vicaire, *Dominique et ses prêcheurs* (2nd ed. Paris: Cerf, 1979); idem, *Histoire de saint Dominique* (2 vols. Paris: Cerf, 1982); Cajetan Esser, *Origins of the Franciscan Order* (Chicago: Franciscan Herald, 1970); Stanislao da Campagnola, *Le origini francescane come problema storiografico* (Perugia: Università degli Studi, 1979); Lazaro Iriarte, *Franciscan History: The Three Orders of St. Francis of Assisi* (Chicago: Franciscan Herlad, 1983); Lawrence C. Landini, *The Causes of the Clericalization of the Order of Friars Minor, 1209-1260, in the Light of Early Franciscan Sources* (Chicago: n. publ, 1968).

[22]See, e.g., Luigi Nanni, "L'Evoluzione storica della parrochia," *Scuola cattolica* 81 (1953) 475-544.

If we take the life of St. Francis as somewhat paradigmatic for the origins of Franciscan ministry, we have a somewhat different picture. It is true that the Franciscan movement cannot be understood apart from the history of the Waldensians and similarly heretical groups, but the direct inspiration for Francis' preaching seems almost certainly to have been the impelling force he felt within himself to speak of the Lord and of His love for all creatures. While the origin of Dominican ministry was a quite specific situation "out there," a need, the origin of Franciscan ministry was more internal to Francis' spirit. The origins of these two ministries were similar, however, in one extremely important regard. Neither of them derived from office.

The origins of the concept of *officium* are ancient, but the most influential description of it came from St. Isidore of Seville in the seventh century. For Isidore it signified the functions connected with major and minor orders, which he understood to be largely ritual and liturgical functions. Gratian and especially later canonists, bearing the burden now of the social and economic legacy of the feudal periods, inextricably linked benefices to *officium*, because benefices were the way those in major and minor orders received their living.[23]

Thus in the clerical state office and benefice were two aspects of the same reality. Even more important from my point of view, however, is that, while office implied the care of souls in some form or other, it did not always in fact so issue. Where it did, furthermore, it looked to stable, established, and well-defined positions, whose functions did not vary from generation to generation.

The Gregorian Reform and its aftermath accelerated and accentuated developments like these in the ministerial apparatus of the Church. In its quest for order in the Church, it aided and abetted closer definition of *officium*, just as it aided and abetted a hierarchical mode of thinking about the clerical state

---

[23]See, e.g., Donald Edward Heintschel, *The Medieval Concept of an Ecclesiastical Office* (Washington: Catholic University of America, 1956); see also Thomas Peter Rausch, *Priesthood and Ministry: From Küng to the Ecumenical Debate* (Ann Arbor: University Microfilms, 1976) esp. 98-144.

that already had grounding in the patristic period with the graduated *cursus honorum* of minor through major orders.

The Gregorian Reform marks the strong articulation, therefore, of what we have come to call the "institutional Church," or, to use Ernst Troeltsch's term, "the church-type." We can still take a hint from Troeltsch's brilliant, though faulty, analysis of the aftermath of the Reform and postulate that the Dominicans and Franciscans represent the "sect-type," an almost inevitable reaction to the church-type.[24] The church-type, whose essence is "its objective institutional character,"[25] would be constituted even in its ministry by order, status, office, and stable functions. In the wake of the feudal and monastic cultures of the early Middle Ages, those constitutive elements of ministry would be further specified as ritual and sacramental.

The sect-type, by definition "a voluntary community,"[26] even in its ministry would be almost the antithesis, evidencing by its flexibility and adaptability the inward inspiration that was its source. Whereas the church-type would find its scriptural warrant in the Pastoral Epistles, the sect-type like the Dominicans and Franciscans would clearly find its warrant in the ministry of Jesus and his first disciples in the Synoptics and in the egalitarian principles in the early chapters of Acts. Francis underscored that egalitarianism when he consistently referred to his group as a *fraternitas*.[27]

For the friars this distinction between the two types cannot be pressed too far, for in many important respects it does not correspond to the facts, nor does it correspond in the main to the friars' self-understanding. "Types" are, after all, artificial constructs designed to make an admittedly too sharp distinction. Neither the Dominicans nor the first followers of Francis defined themselves as against the Church or apart from it, and they found justification for their ministry precisely in the

---

[24] *The Social Teaching of the Christian Churches* 1 (New York: Harper and Row, 1960) 328-82.

[25] Ibid. 338.

[26] Ibid. 339.

[27] See Esser, *Origins* 17-52.

licensing of a bishop, the bishop of Rome. Nonetheless, we must pay attention to the realities that the distinction makes more manifest to us.

It is at this point that the "spirituality" of the early mendicants must enter into consideration. Dominic chose poverty and rejected nominations to the episcopacy so that he might preach in freedom.[28] Asceticism and ministry are thus closely conjoined for the Dominicans. Francis' romance with Lady Poverty may in some ways seems to antedate and be more independent of his own early ministry, if we may thus speak of it, but here too the fusion of spirituality and ministry is early. Both founders were engaged in a ministry of discipleship.[29]

The New Testament, but especially Acts 4:32-37, taught the late-12th and early-13th centuries a great deal about the "apostolic life," for which it showed such great enthusiasm. That apostolic life did not mean only a life of "apostolate" in our sense of the word, but included a life-style modeled on the way the early disciples or "apostles" were supposed to have lived, which to many did not seem to correspond to what they found in the Church of their day. The vows pronounced by the friars, especially the vow of poverty, thus had an important relationship to ministry, even though superficially they might seem to relate only to the ascetical tradition. The apostles, like Jesus, preached, moved around from place to place, shared their goods, and based their relationship to one another on direct personal fellowship. A certain egalitarianism was implied because of the implied recognition of the validity of a variety of charisms in a setting where charism was the foundational value. All these factors, plus others, had impact on the internal structures of the early mendicants, articulated into a system of capitular government—in some contrast to the "monarchy" that was emerging ever more decidedly in the papacy as well as in the episcopacy—and of superiors elected for definite and indefinite terms, quite unlike abbots united to their monasteries

[28]See Vicaire, *Dominique et ses prêcheurs* 222-35.

[29]See Brian E. Daley, "The Ministry of Disciples," *TS* 48 (1987) 605-29, and Avery Dulles, "Imaging the Church for the 1980's" *Thought* 56 (1981) 121-38.

and bishops united to their dioceses until death, and even unlike other clerics united to their benefices in almost the same way.[30]

Another telling difference between the diocesan clergy and the friars developed almost immediately: the concern of the latter for systematic programs of education for their recruits. The friars came into being just as the universities attained their mature organization at the beginning of the 13th century. Although diocesan priests and even monks sometimes attended the universities, the friars had a relationship to them that was systemic. This is not to say that every member of these orders who engaged in ministry attended a university, but rather that explicit programs of education were formulated within them that were based on the same principles that undergirded the university programs.

These programs were created by the internal government of the orders and never suffered any episcopal, or even papal, restraints upon their formulation and implementation. They were the first systematic attempts to formulate and implement programs of education for the clergy that were generally incumbent upon them. The *raison d'être* for such programs was without question the kind of ministry in which the friars principally engaged in the various forms it might take—preaching. Preaching underwent its powerful revival in the 13th century because it figured so clearly in the "apostolic life." It also happened to correspond to the needs of a population that was increasingly urban, more curious and critical, even more literate.[31]

If we should at this point construct a profile of the friar, therefore, we would note that his ministry originated in charism and need, that the minister transcended local lines and moved about "like the apostles," that his ministry consisted to a large degree in preaching and thus required an education, that it related to personal life-style and to the style of governance

[30]See, e.g., Hinnebusch, *Dominican Order*, 1, 217-50; Esser, *Origins* 53-135.

[31]See, e.g., Hinnebusch, *Dominican Order* 1, esp. 3-98: Hilarin Felder, *Geschichte der wissenschaftlichen Studien im Franziskanerorden bis um die Mitte des 13. Jahrhunderts* (Freiburg i/Br.: Herder, 1904).

within the order, which in effect removed him from the governance operative in the church-type. If this profile is inserted into the history of religious life as we now have it, strong continuities emerge because of the ascetical tradition involved. If this profile is inserted into the history of ministry and of church order, however, we perceive a sharp break not only with the preceding monastic and feudal era but to some extent even with the presumably more normative paradigms of, say, the fourth and fifth centuries.

Finally, we must at this point recall that from the beginning both orders enjoyed certain privileges and exemptions from the Holy See, which grew more numerous with passing years. On the surface this fact does not seem terribly remarkable, for it seems to fit into a tradition that goes back to the monastery of Bobbio in the seventh century, but more immediately to the monastery of Cluny in the tenth, when Cluny was taken under the patronage of St. Peter, i.e. the papacy, so that it might be free in its internal affairs from the interference of local patrons— lay and episcopal. This juridical reality gained in clarity and application in the 11th and 12th centuries. What is important for us, however, is not the similarity between the exempt status of Cluny and the later mendicants, but the immense difference.[32]

Cluny was a monastery, and in medieval theory and practice the right of monks to engage in ministry was hotly contested, even forbidden by canon 16 of Lateran Council I, 1123.[33] The "exemption" granted to Cluny was, therefore, in favor of the interior development of the monastery, to try to ensure the election of abbots who would promote its special regimen,

[32]See, e.g., E. Fogliesso, "Exemption des religieux," in *Dictionnaire de droit canonique* 5 (Paris: Letouzey, 1953) 646-65; J. Dubois, "Esenzione monastica," in *Dizionario degli istituti di perfezione* 3 (Rome: Paoline, 1973) 1295-1306; and J Fernández, "Facultà e privilegi negli istituti di perfezione," ibid. 1378-85. See also Burkhard Mathis, *Die Privilegien des Franziskanerordens bis zum Konzil von Vienne (1311)* (Paderborn: F. Schöningh, 1928), exp. 91-115. Even after the publication of the first Code the Jesuits, e.g., issued an *Elenchus praecipuarum facultatum nostris ad auxilium animarum concessarum* (2nd ed. Rome: Curia Praepositi Generalis, 1936).

[33]G. Alberigo et al., eds., *Conciliorum oecumenicorum decreta* (2nd ed.) 193; henceforth *COD*.

especially the long and powerful intercessory liturgies of the monks, which in Cluny were considered their foremost duty.

The similar juridical status granted the Dominicans and Franciscans look, of course, to their internal governance, but the most striking difference from Cluny, Citeaux, and like establishments was that it also looked to ministry. The *ministry* of the friars was exempt from the supervision of the episcopacy, for the friars engaged in ministry in a particular way and, like "the apostles," they transcended local boundaries. This development is a tribute to the stronger papacy that the Gregorian Reform set on its course, as well as to those bishops who supported such exemption for the friars because, whatever its juridical complications, it helped get needed ministry done.

From the viewpoint of church order, of course, this development is astounding. It created in effect a church order (or several church orders) within the great church order, and it did this for the reality to which church order primarily looks—ministry. It is no wonder, therefore, that all through the rest of the Middle Ages well into the 17th century the conflicts between the episcopacy and the religious orders were so many and so characteristically bitter. It *is* a wonder, however, that these various church orders worked together in fact as well as they did and provided such an abundance of ministerial diversity in the Church.

We consistently fail to take account of this *de facto* variety in church order, which goes beyond the familiar patterns of local order and universal order. In the Celtic Church, responsible for so much of the evangelization of barbarian Europe, the abbots governed.[34] In the great monastic centuries, and even beyond, abbots were often the equals of bishops in sacramental powers and in many cases at least their equal in practice, if not in theory, in church order. We forget that, while some 400 bishops celebrated Lateran Council IV, 1215, the greatest and most effective of the medieval councils, their

[34]See, e.g., James Bullock, *The Life of the Celtic Church* (Edinburgh: St. Andrew, 1963); Kathleen Hughes, *The Church in Early Irish Society* (London: Methuen, 1966); and John Ryan, *Irish Monasticism: Origins and Early Development* (Ithaca: Cornell Univ., 1972).

number was dwarfed by the 800 or so abbots who attended—besides some lay magnates and their vicars.[35] The local clergy often had little relationship to the bishop in matters like appointments, and only in the late Middle Ages did urban parishes as such begin to achieve in fact more central status in church life.[36]

The role of monarchs and lay magnates in church order is, of course, of a different character. We must nonetheless recall that, although massively challenged during the Gregorian Reform, it persisted strong and in various forms, with a legitimacy unquestioned by bishops and popes, at least until the French Revolution. Even Pius IX and his collaborators agonized over whether to invite the Catholic monarchs to Vatican Council I, 1870.[37] We must also recall that, despite what we generally read, the monarchs and lay magnates were often, though surely not always, more solicitous for the Church than their clerical counterparts.

The essential point for us, however, is to realize that the story of the mendicants is a story of ministry, and the story of mendicant ministry is inseparable from questions of church order. By the middle of the 13th century, and for some centuries thereafter, the most dynamic, visible, and articulate corps of ministers in the Church did not fall under the jurisdiction, for the most part, of the supervisors of ministry, the local bishops. The mendicants had their warrant from the bishops of Rome. Within that warrant they had a distinctive "order" of their own.

What was innovative here was not the *fact* that the bishop did not have supervision of religious, for that had never been consistently operative in the Middle Ages, or even antiquity. Nor did the innovation consist in exemption as a *juridical* reality, for that had ancient roots. It consisted rather in its being to a great extent an exemption for *ministry*. Local church

---

[35]See Raymonde Foreville, *Latran I, II, III et Latran IV* Paris: L'Orante, 1965) 251-52; see also Georgine Tangl, *Die Teilnehmer an den allgemeinen Konzilien des Mittelalters* (Weimar: H. Böhlaus, 1922) 219-32.

[36]See, e.g., *Handbook of Church History* 3, 566-70.

[37]See Roger Aubert, *Vatican I* (Paris L'Orante, 1964) 50-51.

order for ministry had to reckon with a more universal church order, which itself allowed for further diversities.

The Sixteenth Century

The later Middle Ages were dominated by the ministry of the mendicants—Dominicans and Franciscans, of course, but also Carmelites, Augustinians, and Servites. Although that ministry came under heavy criticism from influential persons like Erasmus and others, its achievements were considerable. It would continue to be, in renewed and somewhat different forms, an extremely powerful influence into the 16th and 17th centuries and well beyond.[38] Nonetheless, in the 16th century a number of important factors converged to effect further changes within Roman Catholicism. Two are especially important for our purposes: the Society of Jesus and the Council of Trent.

If the Jesuits are to be placed in the history of ministry, they must be seen as fundamentally a continuation of the traditions that began with the mendicants and a powerful expansion of them. Nothing is more characteristic of Catholicism in the 16th century than the veritable explosion of ministerial initiatives. In this enterprise the Jesuits were only one force among many, but since they helped create and promote most of these initiatives, they can for our purposes be taken as emblematic.

Although surely not without its debit side, ministry in the Catholic Church in the 16th and 17th centuries was perhaps the most innovative and exciting in history. This well-kept secret began to be revealed only about 20 years ago and still cries for historians to do it justice. "Catholic Reform" of the 16th century was not, therefore, simply a "reform of morals," but a reform of pastoral practice and an immense expansion of its scope.

Perhaps the most striking aspect of 16th-century ministry was the energetic and hardheaded pragmatism that, in con-

[38]See, e.g., John Patrick Donnelly, "Religious Orders of Men," in *Catholicism.*

formity with the medieval tradition, animated it. Whatever seemed to "produce fruit" in souls, whatever met a need, was pursued with creativity and method. Verifications for that generalization can be found in many sources, but perhaps nowhere more consistently than in the 12 volumes of correspondence of St. Ignatius himself.[39] This is all quite a contrast with the more "normative" approach to ministry that prevails today— and with the correlative lassitude of contemporary Catholicism and most mainline churches in many areas of the world.[40]

The dramatic baroque statue of St. Ignatius that stands in the basilica at Loyola, designed by Francisco Vergara in the middle of the 17th century, depicts him in a chasuble, holding a book on which are inscribed the words *Ad majorem Dei gloriam*. The book probably represents the Jesuit *Constitutions*, in which those very words occur so often, and the statue thereby fits Ignatius into the history of religious life. "From Pachomius to Ignatius"!

The chasuble, on the other hand, fits him into the tradition of priesthood. But depicting Ignatius as a priest does not automatically fit him into the history of ministry, which is where he just as deservedly belongs. While Ignatius surely found in the Mass a source of great personal devotion and relied heavily upon its power of impetation, he never considered it as such an instrument of ministry peculiar to his order. Not to exaggerate: there is an implicit co-ordination between priesthood and ministry, between word and sacrament, in early Jesuit sources. Nonetheless, one searches almost in vain in those sources for any mention of priesthood or ordination, whereas the word "ministry" occurs on practically every page. In fact, Vergara would have been even more faithful to the historical sources of Ignatius had he shown him in a pulpit holding a book inscribed *ministerium verbi Dei*. By the time Vergara

[39]*Monumenta Ignatiana: Epistolae et instructiones*, Monumenta Historica Societatis Jesu (12 vols. Madrid: G. Lopez del Horno, 1903-11). See also, e.g., André Ravier, *Ignatius of Loyola and the Founding of the Society of Jesus* (San Francisco: Ignatius, 1987) 359.

[40]See my "Tradition and Traditions" above.

labored, however, such a depiction would have seemed altogether too Protestant.

The fact is, nonetheless, that ministry of the word of God dominates the early Jesuit sources. It is the rubric under which we can gather Ignatius' many activities to be "of help to souls" for the 15 or so years between his conversion and his ordination.[41] It stands in first place in the so-called *Formula of the Institute*, the foundational document that constitutes the essential statement of what the order is all about.[42] Indeed, that phrase can be considered the genus under which almost all the other ministries listed in the *Formula* and in the Jesuit *Constitutions* can be gathered as species. In early Jesuit sources the "herald" model of the Church predominates over the model of the Church as sacrament, to use the well-known constructs of Avery Dulles.[43] (Dulles himself has correctly called attention to the discipleship model that is also operative, perhaps more radically, in those same sources.[44])

By ministry of the word of God the Jesuits of course meant preaching in the usual and conventional sense of the word. But, in continuation with the mendicant tradition, that preaching took place not only during Mass but also in church in the afternoons and other occasions—every day during Advent and Lent. It was also done in the street, hospitals, and other places. By the 17th century a number of new occasions had been created in which sermons played a major role—novenas, Forty Hours, Tre Ore. The presses were jammed with books by Jesuits and others with various "aids" to preachers, and the example and precepts of Cicero and the Fathers of the Church

[41]Ignatius' autobiography has several times been translated into English, most recently by Joseph N. Tylenda, *A Pilgrim's Journey* (Wilmington, Del.: Glazier, 1985).

[42]See *The Constitutions of the Society of Jesus*, tr. George E. Ganss (St. Louis: Institute of Jesuit Sources, 1970) 66 [3]. On the more general issue of priesthood and ministry in the Society of Jesus, see the commendable contribution by William J. Harmless, "Jesuits as Priests, Crisis and Charism," in "Priesthood Today and the Jesuit Vocation," *Studies in the Spirituality of Jesuits* 19, no. 3 (St. Louis: Seminar in Jesuit Spirituality, 1987) 1-47.

[43]*Models of the Church* (Garden City: Doubleday, 1978).

[44]"Imaging the Church" (n. 29 above).

were carefully and sensitively scrutinized for whatever help they might give. For sheer quantity and effort, Catholicism in the late-16th and 17th centuries did not hold second place to any Protestant tradition in preaching.[45]

For the Jesuits, however, ministry of the word of God extended beyond preaching. It included "sacred lectures" on the Bible and theological subjects, that is, series of instructions in church in the afternoons that were a clear forerunner of "adult education." It included catechetical instruction, a ministry that had practically disappeared in the Middle Ages but experienced a great upsurge in the 16th century. It included exhortations to religious communities and teaching local clergy about "cases of conscience." It even included "spiritual conversation" on the word of God among individuals and in small groups, on either a planned or spontaneous basis.

All these forms of the ministry of the word of God were integrated into one of the most important ministerial instruments that 16th-century Catholicism created: the "mission" to small villages and hamlets. The Middle Ages knew nothing like them, nor did the patristic era. These missions to the rural poor were excellently organized pastoral strategies, in which were combined preaching, catechesis, adult education, folk piety, and conversion to godly ways in the sacraments of Eucharist and especially of penance. The missionaries arrived at a locality in groups of two to eight, generally stayed for four to six weeks, and had clearly-formulated goals. By the 17th century the missions, these Catholic "revivals," had proved so successful that they also began to be directed to towns and cities. The new orders—especially the Jesuits, Capuchins, and Vincentians—took the lead.[46]

Few words are more familiar to us today than "mission," for even businesses sometimes profess to have one. Until the

---

[45]See my contribution "Preaching," to appear in the encyclopedia of Jesuit history now being compiled at the Jesuit Historical Institute, Rome. See also Peter Bayley, "Preaching," in *Catholicism.*

[46]See, e.g., my "Preaching," and Jean Delumeau, *Catholicism between Luther and Voltaire: A New View of the Counter-Reformation* (Philadelphia: Westminster, 1977) 189-94.

16th century, however, it was practically restricted even in religious circles to describing realities of the Blessed Trinity. The Jesuits helped recover and popularize the word to describe how their ministries were to be made operative, in imitation of the "sending" of the apostles, and in early Jesuit literature "mission" is sometimes synonymous with "journey" and "pilgrimage."[47] Not by stable office but by mission, or by perception of need, did one undertake one's ministry. By the 17th century the word had been taken up by other religious groups and entered our common vocabulary.

The best publicized, though not necessarily the best studied, ministry of the Jesuits was the network of schools they established, which by the early-17th century numbered over 400 spread around the globe. Despite the role the Church played in medieval institutions of learning, i.e. the universities, neither antiquity nor the Middle Ages knew anything like the "church-related" schools created by the Jesuits and others in the 16th and 17th centuries. Even these astounding facts are not so impressive, for our purposes, as the change in mentality they indicate. For the first time in history, conducting schools and teaching in them had now become a form of ministry, formally considered such in the Jesuit documents and in those of other orders and congregations that shared with them in the general enthusiasm.[48] A 16th-century source captured that enthusiasm in a few words: *Institutio puerorum, renovatio mundi.*[49]

By formalizing and putting method into certain religious practices as old as Christianity itself, or older, the orders and congregations of the 16th century in effect created new ministries and instruments of ministry in the area we sometimes today dub "ministries of interiority." Outstanding among these was the retreat, which we can with a certain qualification say

[47]See my "To Travel"; Mario Scaduto, "La strada e i primi Gesuiti," *Archivum historicum Societatis Jesu* 40 (1971) 323-90; and esp. F. Bourdeau, "Le vocabulaire de la mission," *Parole et mission* 3 (1960) 9-27.

[48]See, e.g., Paul Grendler, "Schools, Seminaries, and Catechetical Instruction," in *Catholicism.*

[49]Said by Juan Bonifacio, S.J., as quoted in John W. Donahue, *Jesuit Education: An Essay on the Foundation of Its Idea* (New York: Fordham Univ., 1963) 186.

was created by the Spiritual Exercises and the practice that followed upon them. The practice of spiritual direction became so widespread among the devout and reflection upon it entered such a new phase that it is almost a different reality from what the Middle Ages knew. The printing press offered, of course, occasion to continue all the genres known in the Middle Ages, but the upsurge in quantity of books of "spiritual reading," as well as apologetics against the Protestants in certain areas of Europe, indicates a new ministry in the making. The principal agents of all these changes were the religious orders and congregations.[50]

The Jesuits, like others, were also active in "social" ministries, founding and promoting programs or houses to assist catechumens, reformed prostitutes, the poor and the ill, orphans and others. Of special note here is the concern to engage laymen and laywomen in these projects. These laypersons were often asked to finance them, but, in keeping with late-medieval traditions, they also were expected to bear primary responsibility for their ongoing operation.[51]

The list of new or almost new ministries that the 16th century brought into being could be extended further and refined, but it is even more important to point out a general feature of much of it that finds clear articulation in the Jesuit documents. This feature concerns the persons among whom religious priests exercised their ministry. The list given in the Jesuit *Formula* is authoritative: ". . . among the Turks or any other infidels, even those who live in the region called the Indies, or among any heretics whatever, or schismatics, or any of the faithful."[52] The "missions" to infidels outside Europe date back to the mendicants in the 13th century, with St. Francis himself preaching before El-Kamil, the Sultan of Egypt. These missions powerfully expanded in the "Age of Discovery" in the 16th century, when the mendicants were now joined by the

---

[50]See my "Early Jesuit Spirituality: Spain and Italy," forthcoming in *Christian Spirituality* 3, ed. Louis Dupré (New York: Crossroad).

[51]See, e.g., Ravier, *Loyola* 359.

[52]*Constitutions* 68 [4].

Jesuits and others. Moreover, the Reformation created a situation that gave special urgency to ministry among "heretics and schismatics."

Jerónimo Nadal, the contemporary and best interpreter of St. Ignatius, reduced the Jesuit list in effect to *anybody* in *need*, especially those who are neglected and have nobody to minister to them.[53] Thus Nadal interprets the Jesuits' famous Fourth Vow. That vow to go anywhere in the world, if sent, in order to do ministry dramatizes the basic assumption that Jesuit ministry is perhaps as far removed from the pattern of stable and local *officium* as it was possible to get. It seems clear, in fact, that in the Jesuit documents the itinerant Paul is the implicit model for ministry.[54] "From *Paul* to Ignatius" would be the title of the appropriate book on the subject.

Peter also figures in the vow, in fact more explicitly. This vow about doing ministry anywhere in the world specifies the bishop of Rome as the one who would send the Jesuit on this mission. In Jesuit sources the formality under which the pope is viewed in this context is precisely his more universal responsibilty and, presumably, vision. That is, he will see beyond the local Church—or even beyond the Church altogether, for he should be more aware of infidels, heretics, pagans and schismatics. The superior general of the Society of Jesus for the same reasons has the same kind of authority to "send" any of his subjects anywhere.

The Fourth Vow serves another function important for our purposes. It provides a clear indication that religious profession was not a link simply with "Pachomius" but also with ministry— even though that latter link was often not explicitly expressed in the formula of the vows or, as with the Jesuits, not generally understood in that way. Ignatius once called that vow "the

[53]See my "To Travel."

[54]Nadal in fact states: "Petrus firmitatem et directionem, Paulus nobis ministerium in Societate nostra significat, et adiuvat uterque ut Ecclesiae Princeps" (*Orationis observationes*, ed. Miguel Nicolau [Rome: Institutum Historicum Societatis Jesu, 1964] 151 [41]).

principle and principal foundation" of the Society.[55] He did not exaggerate. Other religious institutes, in the Middle Ages and of course in modern times, have in fact also had "special" vows that related in similarly direct fashion to ministry.[56] If the Jesuits embody and symbolize one aspect of Catholic Reform in the 16th century, the Council of Trent does the same for another. In 1975 Hubert Jedin completed his massive, masterful history of the Council, the culmination of a lifetime of research and of training students in the history of every aspect of the "Tridentine era."[57] We are now better informed about the Council than we have ever been. Given the immense obstacles we now see the Council had to overcome during the 18 years over which it stretched, its achievements seem even more brilliant.

This research has also, however, made us more aware of the limitations of the Council and has not yet answered every question about its immediate impact upon the Church. In other words, now that we have so much solid information about Trent, we are faced even more squarely with questions about how to assess it.[58] In this task, especially as it pertains to our purposes, it is important to recall again the two stated aims of the Council, which in fact continued to guide it through its tumultuous course: (1) "to confirm doctrine" and (2) "to reform morals."[59] In actual fact, both of these aims admitted further specification. "To confirm doctrine" meant to deal not with all doctrines but only those attacked by the Protestants and, as things almost inevitably worked out, practically in the terms of the attack. "To reform morals" was taken as synon-

---

[55]See my "The Fourth Vow" and Burkhart Schneider, "Nuestro Principio y principal Fundamento: Zum historischen Verständnis des Papstgehorsamsgelübdes,"*Archivum historicum Societatis Jesu* 25 (1956) 488-513.

[56]See, e.g., Johannes Günter Gerhartz, *Insuper Promitto. . . ": Die feierlichen Sondergelübde katholischen Orden* (Rome: Gregoriana, 1966).

[57]*Geschichte des Konzils von Trient* (4 vols. in 5. Freiburg i/Br.: Herder, 1950-75). Only the first two volumes have been translated into English: *A History of the Council of Trent* (London: Thomas Nelson, 1957-61).

[58]See, e.g., Giuseppe Alberigo, "The Council of Trent," in *Catholicism.*

[59]Sessio IV (April 8, 1546), COD 664.

ymous with the older phrase "reform of the Church," which had by 1545 become too dangerous and ambiguous. Trent undertook "to reform morals" through certain juridical changes. Masked therefore under "reform of morals" were issues of church order, little aware though we have been of their importance until recently.

All this means that in a period in which Roman Catholicism was experiencing an explosion of ministerial initiatives that in their intensity and creativity were for any given period almost unprecedented, Trent took little or no notice. Part of the explanation lies in the fact that many of these initiatives were happening contemporaneously with the Council and came fully into their own only after the Council ended. But the more fundamental reason is the agenda of the Council itself. Trent mandated a catechism, but has not a word to say about retreats, spiritual reading, spiritual direction, social ministries, "missions"—even about evangelization of the various "Indies" that had been under way for a half century and would eventually change the face of Catholicism. One catches in Trent only the slightest mention of schools and "adult education."[60] Trent took notice of the printing press in its concern about the Index of Forbidden Books (also a creation of the 16th century), but never proposed that the press might become an instrument of ministry.[61]

Jedin judges that the vision underlying Trent's many decrees on reform was to transform bishops "from feudatories into pastors."[62] That is, from exploiters of benefices into ministers. One would expect to find, therefore, a great deal in Trent about *ministries*, but, as I indicated above, one finds very little. Some of this blindness surely stems from certain assumptions about the unchanging character of the Church—and therefore of its ministries—that blinds one to changes actually taking

[60]See Sessio V (June 17, 1546), ibid. 667-70. On this rather ineffective decree, see Jedin, *Trent* 2, 99-124.

[61]Sessio XVIII (Feb. 26, 1562), COD 723-24, and Sessio XXV (Dec. 3, 1563), ibid. 797.

[62]With Giuseppe Alberigo, *La figura ideale del vescovo secondo la Riforma cattolica* (2nd ed. Brescia: Paideia, 1985).

place. It is not at all clear, indeed, that even the creators of the new ministries were fully aware of how innovative they actually were.

Preaching is one ministry that receives attention in Trent, although the amount of space actually devoted to it is small in comparison with the totality of the Council's decrees and canons. Trent's designation of preaching as the *praecipuum munus* of the bishop had great impact upon Carlo Borromeo and a few other reforming bishops, and hence contributed significantly to the general revival of this form of ministry of the word of God.[63] If we lacked this subsequent history about Borromeo and his likes, however, the lines from Trent on preaching could almost escape our notice. Moreover, Trent seemed to mean "preaching" in a most conventional sense and gives no hints as to how even this ministry might be revived by new methods and techniques, subjects that in fact had already been greatly discussed "in the field" for decades.[64]

Since Trent felt obliged by the Protestant attack to deal with all the sacraments, it had occasion to deal with ministry when it considered the sacrament of orders.[65] In that decree, however, ministry is in effect not mentioned. For Trent the sacrament of orders relates to office and hierarchy, and it confers the power to administer the sacraments, most especially to confect the Eucharist.

Two features of the decree deserve comment. First, the correlation that we saw in Isidore among *officium*, ritual, and both major and minor orders had persisted up through Trent. In answering the Protestant challenge to the sacrament of

---

[63]Sessio XXIV (Nov. 11, 1563), canon 4, COD 763. On preaching see also Sessio V (June 17, 1546), ibid. 667-70. On Borromeo see my "Saint Charles Borromeo and the *Praecipuum episcoporum munus:* His Place in the History of Preaching," in *San Carlo Borromeo: Catholic Reform and Ecclesiastical Politics in the Second Half of the Sixteenth Century,* ed. John Headley (Washington, D.C.: University Press of America, 1988), pp. 139-57.

[64]See, e.g., my "Content and Rhetorical Form in Sixteenth-Century Treatises on Preaching," in *Renaissance Eloquence*, ed. James J. Murphy (Berkeley: Univ. of California, 1983) 238-52, and now especially Debora Shuger, *Sacred Rhetoric: The Christian Grand Style in the English Renaissance* (Princeton Univ., 1988).

[65]Sessio XXIII (July 15, 1563), COD 742-44.

orders, Trent in the process accepted, as it almost inevitably had to, older formulations and assumptions about the nature of priesthood. Secondly, the decree falls among the *doctrinal* decrees of Trent. Thus, what Trent is dealing with is the *idea* of what orders or priesthood is, without any attempt to correlate that idea with the living reality. This dichotomy between doctrine and practice manifests itself even in Trent, for in its *reform* decrees preaching and pastoral governance were taken into account.[66]

Although the correlation office-orders-ritual has even older roots, the specific identification of priesthood with the power to confect the Eucharist received a classic formulation with Saint Peter Damian, one of the Gregorian reformers of the 11th century.[67] Damian's identification is not surprising, since he lived in the monastic age that for all practical purposes knew no ministry, only liturgy. The model of the Church as sacrament never found fuller expression in social reality, for instance, than in the elaborate liturgies of Cluny.

More surprising is that Aquinas' *Summa theologiae* two centuries later in effect repeats the identification—so strong is the force of tradition—when it speaks of the sacrament of orders. No correlation is made with Thomas' own priesthood as a member of a religious order whose priests by definition were "preachers."[68] It is significant that only when Thomas

---

[66]See Schillebeeckx, *Human Face* 197-201, and the perceptive article, with ample bibliography, by Severino Dianich, "La teologia del presbiterato al Concilio di Trento," *Scuola cattolica* 99 (1971) 331-58. See also Alexandre Ganoczy, "'Splendours and Miseries' of the Tridentine Doctrine of Ministries," in *Concilium* 80 (New York: Herder and Herder, 1972) 75-86.

[67]See his *Liber gratissimus*, c. 15 (PL 145, 118). See also Yves Congar, *L'Eglise: De s. Augustin à l'époque moderne* (Paris: Cerf, 1970) 170-71, and his "Modèle monastique et modèle sacerdotal en occident de Grégoire VII (1073-1085) à Innocent III (1198)," in his *Etudes d'ecclésiologie médiévale* (London: Variorum, 1983) IX. Congar's observation is apposite (158): "Il me semble que les XIIIᵉ-XVᵉ siècles aient été une époque essentiellement 'cléricale,' non au sens des problèmes politiques qui sont liés au cléricalisme, mais en ce sense qu'alors le Catholicisme est essentiellement religion du sacrement."

[68]Suppl., qq. 34-40. Although the Supplement was not written by Thomas, it generally represents his thinking on a given issue, and even more surely that of his age: see, e.g., *Sum. theol.* 3, 82, 1.

discusses religious life does he deal with ministries—in particular the ministries of preaching and hearing confessions, which he notes that both religious and "presbyteri curati" do.[69] When he treats of bishops, he recognizes in them an office grounded on the care of souls, but in effect he identifies this care more with *regimen* than with any direct ministry.[70] What is especially pertinent for us, however, is that Aquinas correlates ministry with certain forms of religious life rather than with the sacrament of orders per se.

The documents of the Council of Trent advert to the fact that religious were doing ministry, and tried to assure that this ministry be properly supervised. Nonetheless, the specific decree "Concerning Regulars and Nuns" deals practically exclusively with discipline internal to the orders and their houses, i.e. with matters pertaining ultimately to the personal holiness of the members, which betrays a mentality that will still view religious as essentially in the Pachomian tradition.[71]

At Lateran IV in the early 13th century the abbots far outnumbered the bishops. At Trent there were practically no abbots present, and for all practical purposes the only voting members were bishops. These simple facts already suggest that Trent would be a bishops' council, and, as I indicated earlier, a large number of reform decrees looked directly to the episcopacy—in an effort to "reform their morals" but also to enhance their authority. Trent knew no other way to accomplish these two goals than by creating and/or implementing certain juridical structures.

Were these goals for the episcopacy ever accomplished? In the long, long run there were surely some successes, and at least "on the books" episcopal authority in many areas was more fully postulated than ever before. As is well known, however, the authority that the Council in fact most strongly promoted, although only indirectly and beyond its intention,

---

[69]*Sum. theol.* 3, 188, 4; see also 2-2, 184, 6 and 8.

[70]Ibid. 2-2, 185. He does, however, implicitly recognize preaching, ibid., a. 6, and 2.

[71]Sessio XXV (Dec. 3-4, 1563), COD 776-84.

was that of the papacy.[72] Once again here we see how misleading official documents can be, for the authority of the papacy was never directly treated at Trent and, indeed, debate over the precise nature and extent of that authority came within a hair's breadth of utterly destroying the Council in 1563.[73]

As Trent treated of bishops and tried to strengthen their authority in their dioceses, it attempted to do the same for pastors and their parishes. These latter institutions were, after all, the articulation of the diocese. This aspect of the Council has generally received little notice, for to our contemporary way of thinking it seems to say little that is noteworthy, so generally has it been accepted. John Bossy has in recent years, however, repeatedly called attention to this phenomenon and has heavily criticized it for imposing on the Church a pattern of "parochial conformity." Such an effectively prescriptive pattern was unknown in the Middle Ages, when the pastoral machinery was more complex, variegated, and, according to Bossy, more integrated into the "natural" fabric of life.[74] Bossy sees the change as ultimately detrimental to religious practice.

Just when and why a pattern of "parochial conformity" took hold are questions that are not easy to answer; yet the answers must range beyond the legislation of Trent in order to be adequate. However, there can be no doubt, in my opinion, that by its decrees the Council set the Church on a long journey that by the 20th century meant that when people thought of "church" they thought of "parish," when they thought of "priest" they thought of "pastor." In the Middle Ages being enrolled in one's confraternity was sufficient to ensure Christian burial, just as that enrollment provided spiritual nourishment in the company of one's peers and professional "kin"

---

[72]See, e.g., Alberigo, "Trent," and his "L'Episcopato nel cattolicismo post-tridentino," *Cristianesimo nella storia* 6 (1985) 71-91.

[73]See Hubert Jedin, *Crisis and Closure of the Council of Trent* (London: Sheed and Ward, 1967).

[74]See esp. his "The Counter Reformation and the People of Catholic Europe," *Past and Present*, no. 47 (May 1970) 51-70. See also now the important article by Alberigo, "The Local Church."

during life. That is to say, from the sixth century even until long after the Council of Trent the parish church was only one element in a vast and lumbering array of other institutions like monasteries, priories, shrines, manor chapels, oratories, guilds, confraternities, third orders, sodalities, schools, and collegiate churches (to which list "retreat houses" would at a certain point be added) where in one way or another Christians satisfied their devotion. These institutions were like the sect-type itself, "voluntary." Perhaps for that reason they were able to evoke engagement and thus help impart to medieval Christianity such vitality. The shift in church order that Trent legislated and promoted in this regard would obviously have immense impact, in time, on how and where persons would normatively—even obligatorily—be ministered unto and on what religious opportunities would generally be open to them. The Code of Canon Law of 1917, and again of 1983, developed along the same lines.

Vatican Council II

After Trent it was not until four centuries later that a council would once again deal with episcopacy, priesthood, and religious life. Vatican II believed itself to be in continuity with Trent on these issues, and to a considerable extent it surely was. In some ways, however, the differences are more striking than the similarities. The fathers of Vatican II spoke out of their experience of the Church of the 20th century, which, partly because of the long-range impact of Trent, was much different from the Church of the sixteenth. Moreover, the fathers of Vatican II, practically all of whom were bishops or their equivalent, had through their theologians access to perspectives, especially some historical perspectives, that Trent lacked. From these two frameworks of past and present they constructed models of episcopacy, priesthood, and religious life. These models or ideals they presented as such in clear, though often quite general, terms.

Precisely in the terms, or rhetoric, lies one of the great

differences between Trent and Vatican II.[75] In its reform decrees Trent's language is invariably juridical. To discover the "ideal bishop" of the fathers at Trent, one must extract and reconstruct it from hundreds of juridical details. Vatican II, on the other hand, presented goals and idealized models. These goals and ideals were generally painted in the broadest possible terms, so as to include all. Two problems arise, however, from this approach. First, the ideal, general though it may be, does not always seem adequate to every situation. Secondly, these ideals sometimes imply or allow certain assumptions about church order or changes within it, but do not clearly state them. These two problems have sometimes been rendered more obvious by official documents issued after the Council than they were in the decrees of the Council itself, so these must also be given some consideration if we are to understand the present situation. For the sake of clarity and conciseness, however, I will gather what I have to say under the rubric of the documents of the Council that treat most directly of the issues that concern us.

Perfectae caritatis has provoked much discussion and even controversy over how to implement its injunction to religious to make changes in their institutes while remaining faithful to their original charism.[76] The sources for the disagreements over how to interpret the decree in this regard are many and complex, but surely one of the most fundamental is the very framework in which the Council presents religious life. It is the framework of the three vows. It is the framework of the personal search for spiritual perfection (presumably enhanced in some cases with the additional adornment of ministry). It is

---

[75]See above pp. 111-15.

[76]For the history of the decree and commentaries, see *L'Adaptation et la rénovation de la vie religieuse: Décret "Perfectae Caritatis,"* ed. J. M. R. Tillard and Y. Congar (Paris: Cerf, 1967), and Friedrich Wulf, "Decree on the Appropriate Renewal of Religious Life," in *Commentary on the Documents of Vatican II,* ed. Herbert Vorgrimler (5 vols. New York: Herder and Herder, 1967-69) 2, 301-70. Two especially important treatments of the general problem are John M. Lozana, *Discipleship: Towards an Understanding of Religious Life* (Chicago: Claret Center, 1980), and Sandra M. Schnieders, *New Wineskins: Re-imaging Religious Life Today* (New York: Paulist, 1986).

the framework of from-Pachomius-to-Ignatius. Yet today we must ask: Does the traditional way of *interpreting* religious life fully correspond to the *tradition* of religious life? Of the 25 sections of *Perfectae caritatis*, only two (nos. 8 and 20) are devoted to ministry.[77] Yet the Dominicans and the Jesuits—to name only some of the best-known and clearest examples—were founded precisely to do ministry, indeed, to do ministry in quite special ways. But the framework in which *Perfectae caritatis* was conceived makes it impossible for it to take adequate account of this absolutely basic consideration. The postconciliar *Essentials of Religious Life* makes the problem even more manifest.[78] That document has been criticized for reducing religious life to a monastic model. The more general weakness, however, is that it implies that religious life, as we have generally known it since the 13th century, can be reduced to "the three vows." Absolutely constitutive though these vows are, they do not directly express the full reality.

Presbyterorum ordinis has not received much attention since the Council, but it is an important document.[79] Unlike Trent, it makes a clear correlation between priesthood and ministry. It also attempts, not altogether successfully, to break the identification of priesthood with confection of the Eucharist and states that "it is the first task of priests" to preach the gospel.[80] Moreover, while utilizing the triad priest-prophet-king to describe the function of "presbyters," it redefines those terms to integrate them into a more collaborative perspective than they directly indicate.[81]

[77]See the comments on these two sections by Wulf, *Commentary* 2, 352-53.

[78]The English text is in *Origins*, 13 (1983) 133-42, document dated May 31, 1983.

[79]For the history of the document and commentary, see *Les prêtres: Décrets "Presbyterorum ordinis" et "Optatam totius,"* ed. J. Frisque et Y. Congar (Paris: Cerf, 1968), and Friedrich Wulf et al., "Decree on the Ministry and Life of Priests," *Commentary* 4, 183-297. See also *Los presbiteros: A los diez años de "Presbyterorum ordinis,"* Teología del sacerdocio, no. 7 (Burgos: Ediciones Aldecoa, 1975), and Brian Charles Foley, "De cura animarum: A Voice for the Priesthood," in *Vatican II Revisited by Those Who Were There*, ed. Alberic Stacpoole (Minneapolis: Winston, 1986) 255-69.

[80]*PO*, no. 4. For a detailed comparison of *PO* with Trent, see *Les Prêtres 193-232.*

[81]See *PO*, nos. 4-6. On the origins of the triad, see now Peter J. Drilling, "The Priest, Prophet and King Trilogy,"to appear in *Eglise et théologie* (1988).

Nonetheless, despite its many fine features and the good intentions that prompted it, religious must not be unmindful of the challenges it delivers to them. The document presents an ideal and a model of priesthood—a construct. This construct is based, first, on the analogue of the contemporary diocesan clergy. Secondly, the normative model that is operative, I suggest, is the patristic Church, as is somewhat indicated by the number of references to patristic documents.[82] The Church that Ambrose and Augustine knew was a close-knit community of clergy around their bishop, ministering by word and sacrament to a stable community of the faithful in the rather-well-defined world of the Christian emperors. That Church and world are, however, far different from anything we have known since at least the sixth century even, in my opinion, up today. From what biblical scholars tell us, it also seems to be different in many respects from the Church, or churches, that we find in parts of the New Testament.

As I mentioned earlier, *Presbyterorum ordinis* makes three basic assumptions about the priest-minister.[83] The first concerns the place and structure of ministry. Although it is not always explicitly stated, the document presupposes as normative that the priest-minister will deal with a *stable* community, in which, moreover, a regular rhythm of liturgies of word and sacrament will be celebrated. The word "parish" is seldom mentioned, but the idea is omnipresent. At least by implication, the parish is normative for ministry.

The second assumption is almost a corollary. The stable community is composed of the *faithful.* Some notice is taken of what the Council elsewhere says about evangelization, ecumenism, and the manifold issues raised about "the Church in the modern world," but it is almost perfunctory.[84] The priest-minister of *Presbyterorum ordinis* will deal with the faithful, and his training as proposed in *Optatam totius* will be designed

---

[82]See *Les Prêtres 376-77.*

[83]These three assumptions also clearly undergird *Lumen gentium,* no. 28, which was foundational for *PO.* See *Les prêtres* 138.

[84]*PO,* no. 4, best indicates awareness of the necessity of evangelization.

to prepare him precisely for that flock.

The third assumption relates to church order. The priest-minister is in hierarchical communion with his bishop. The remote model from which this assumption derives seems, again, to be the patristic Church, and it suggests an appealing collaboration and co-ordination between the bishop and his clergy. But we must not miss how repeatedly this document, as well as others, returns to the relationship between bishop and priest, almost to the point of defining the priest-minister through that relationship. *Optatam totius* goes so far as to speak of the priest as participating in "the hierarchical priesthood of Christ," an intriguing notion.[85]

At this point it is hardly necessary to point out how difficult it is to reconcile these assumptions with the traditions of ministry in most of the religious orders. That ministry was not structured with an eye to a local and stable community, as symbolized by the parish, but transcended diocese and even nation—"to go anywhere in the world," as the Jesuit *Constitutions* say. Although all the orders ministered to the faithful, they had a special interest in heretics, schismatics, infidels. It was not without good grounding in tradition, for instance, that Pope John Paul II in his allocution opening the 33rd General Congregation of the Society of Jesus, September 2, 1983, especially commended to the Jesuits ministries like "ecumenism, the deeper study of relations with non-Christian religions, and the dialogue of the Church with cultures," and "the evangelizing action of the Church to promote justice, connected with world peace."[86]

Even among the faithful, religious orders and congregations have tended to have a special interest in those whom the ordinary ministry of the Church for one reason or another failed to reach: orphans, young vagrants, prostitutes, the "alienated"—or, on the other hand, those laity seeking to devote themselves to God and their neighbor in more challenging and unconventional ways. Moreover, their "instruments of

[85]*OT*, no. 2, "ad Christi Sacerdotium hierarchicum."

[86]This English version is found in *Documents of the 33rd General Congregation of the Society of Jesus* (St. Louis: Institute of Jesuit Sources, 1984) 77-84, esp. 81-82.

ministry" showed an ingenuity that carried them beyond the rhythm of word and sacrament in the usual senses of those terms. Finally, the priests of the great orders had no hierarchical relationship with the ordinary of the place, but had a fraternal, or capitular, or "sect-type" relationship with their own ordinary.

This brings us to *Christus Dominus*, the decree on the pastoral office of bishops in the Church.[87] As adjusted to the bishops, the same three assumptions are operative as in *Presbyterorum ordinis*. The bishop presides over a local community, of the faithful, in hierarchical communion with the bishop of Rome. The convergence of these three elements manifests in a striking degree certain elements of the "church-type," for it projects a ministry based on office, on well-defined and normative functions, on authority that is clearly articulated and regulatory, and on the maintenance of faith and order. Although these elements have been traditionally associated with the office of bishop, they had never before been pulled together in precisely the same way and, of course, never before presented to the Church with the authority of a council. In comparison with these broad strokes in Vatican II, the "ideal bishop" of Trent seems lost in a myriad of juridical detail.

Nonetheless, underneath what often seem to be bland generalizations, *Christus Dominus* deals with church order in just as significant a way as the legislation of Trent. It projects a vision of church order that has raised a number of complex questions, as our newspapers seem to testify almost daily, but that in a number of instances seem fraught with special consequences for religious. The document states, for instance: "All priests, whether diocesan or religious, share and exercise with the bishop the one priesthood of Christ. They are thus constituted providential cooperators of this episcopal order."[88]

---

[87]For the history of the document and commentary, see W. Onclin et al., *La charge pastorale des évêques: Décret "Christus Dominus"* (Paris: Cerf, 1969), and Klaus Mörsdorf, "Decree on the Bishops' Pastoral Office in the Church," *Commentary* 2, 165-300.

[88]*CD*, no. 28. The second sentence is taken from the Preface of the ordination of priests. See the important qualifications by Mörsdorf, *Commentary*, 2, 256.

The paragraph goes on to assert: "The diocesan clergy have, however, a [the] primary role in the care of souls because, being incardinated in or appointed to a particular church, they are wholly dedicated in its service to the care of a particular section of the Lord's flock, and accordingly form one priestly body and one family of which the bishop is father."[89] Pastors of parishes hold first place among the collaborators with the bishops in the care of souls.[90]

If "care of souls" (*cura animarum*) is taken in the technical and canonical sense, nothing new is being said here, for in that sense *cura animarum* refers to the office that has traditionally belonged to the diocesan clergy, especially pastors. Nonetheless, the groundwork seems to have been laid for a generalization made later about religious priests that relates priesthood as such to the episcopacy: "Religious priests, who have been raised to the priesthood to be prudent co-operators with the episcopal order, ... may be said in a certain sense to belong to the clergy of the diocese inasmuch as they share in the care of souls and in the practice of apostolic works under the authority of the bishop."[91] Just a few lines later a crucial and logical consequence is drawn for religious, and probably more directly for their superiors: "Furthermore, religious should comply promptly and faithfully with the requests or desires of bishops when they are asked to undertake a greater share in the ministry of salvation (*salutis humanae ministerium*)."[92] "Ministry of salvation" seems to have become here a synonym for "care of souls."

The following propositions, though crudely put, summarize this aspect of *Christus Dominus*. There is one priesthood,

[89]*CD*, no. 28. The Latin seems clearly to indicate the definite article for English, whereas the edition by Flannery (580) employs the indefinite: "In animarum autem cura procuranda primas partes habent sacerdotes diocesani .... "

[90]*CD*, no. 30: "Praecipua autem ratione Episcopi cooperatores sunt parochi, quibus, tamquam pastoribus propriis, animarum cura committitur in determinata dioecesis parte sub illius auctoritate."

[91]*CD*, no. 34. The convoluted explanation that Mörsdorf gives of no. 34 indicates the complexity of the issues (*Commentary* 2, 266-68).

[92]*CD*, no. 35.

which cannot be defined apart from the "episcopal order."
That priesthood is concerned with the "care of souls," which
has meant and still seems to mean primarily the ministry of
pastors of parishes under the bishop. Although religious orders
of priests have in former times on occasion been forbidden
such "care of souls," or like the Jesuits, have themselves explicitly renounced it in favor of other ministries,[93] they now
seem by virtue of their ordination almost to be destined for it.
There seems to be, moreover, at least a suggestion that all
"ministry of salvation" is reducible to "care of souls."

I would maintain, therefore, that for all their merit *Christus
Dominus, Presyterorum ordinis,* and *Optatam totius* do not
take into sufficient account the tradition of ministry and priesthood in the religious orders. The Council could not take this
tradition properly into account because the history of it had
not yet been done, or at least not done in a helpful way, for
reflection on the nature of religious life was always encased in
the from-Pachomius-to-Ignatius framework. This means that
in effect the Council had little choice but to reduce religious
life to the practice of certain forms of spirituality, some more
"active" than others. When religious do ministry, they may
enhance it with a special "spirit," but for all practical purposes
they function as diocesan priests.

Confirmation of this interpretation can be seen in what the
Council says about the exempt status of some religious. It
asserts that the privilege of exemption from the jurisdiction of
bishops "relates primarily to the internal organization of the
institutes ... [so that] the perfection of religious life [is]
promoted."[94] That was surely the sole purpose of the first
exemptions of Cluny in the tenth century, but beginning with
the 13th the most impressive privileges of the orders related
directly to ministry. The great orders of mendicants, for instance, each had its so-called *mare magnum,* their comprehensive grants of pastoral prerogatives. Moreover, even the
"internal organization" of these and subsequent orders was

[93]*Constitutions,* nos. 324, 325, 588.
[94]*CD,* no. 35.

directed to a large extent to ministry. The programs of study and formation themselves were not directed to "the love of learning and the desire for God" as in the monastic tradition, but towards more effective ministry.[95]

Conclusion

By this point I hope to have established at least that there are other possible ways of looking at the history of ministry and priesthood, of church order and reform, of spirituality and religious life itself. I would, moreover, contend that our more systematic reflection on these issues will be significantly hampered, even blocked, until we devise for them more adequate historical frameworks. Two items on this agenda are most urgent. First, we must try to achieve a better integration among themselves of all these aspects of church life which until now have to a large extent been treated separately and, in some cases, almost as if they had no relationship to one another. Such an integration would take special note of the millennium and a half between the end of the patristic period and the opening of Vatican II.

The second item would be to study all these aspects most diligently as they manifest themselves in the *life* of the Church. In other words, we must not look so exclusively to what the Church said about these issues as to how it has in fact *acted*. Besides its other merits, such a shift would bring scholarship into better conformity with what the Council itself implicitly enjoined with its profound statement in *Dei verbum*: "What was handed on by the apostles comprises everything that serves to make the People of God live their lives in holiness and increase their faith. In this way the Church in her doctrine, *life*, and worship perpetuates and transmits to every generation *all*

---

[95]See my "The Houses of Study of Religious Orders and Congregations: An Historical Sketch," in Katarina Schuth's study of the future of Roman Catholic theologates, forthcoming (Wilmington, Del: Glazier, 1988).

that she herself is, all that she believes."[96]

We must, in any case, reckon that even religious geniuses like Dominic, Francis, and Ignatius may not have been fully capable of expressing what they were doing or hoped to do, so that that expression must confront their actions in the long context of the traditions in which they moved. For all their merits, to give another instance, the decrees of the Council of Trent do not tell us everything we need to know about ministry and priesthood in the 16th century. In fact, on these points the decrees are unwittingly but decidedly misleading.

Studies along the lines I am proposing are not just an academic exercise. I believe that they have important repercussions not only on how "regular priests" think about themselves, and therefore are trained and pursue their ministries, but on other groups and on the Church at large. For all the confusion and complexity that encumber the issues treated in this article, confusion and complexity so profound that I have hardly been able to touch the surface, some rather specific conclusions have emerged.[97] In closing, the following considerations seem to me especially pertinent.

1. In the vast majority of orders and congregations founded since the 13th century, ministry has been at the center of their self-understanding. Definitions and descriptions of religious life that fail to take full account of this indisputable fact are, no matter what their other merits, misleading and harmful.

2. There have been at least since that time two quite distinct traditions of ministry that have given shape to the reality of priesthood in the Church. Both can claim legitimacy in the New Testament and in the long history of the Church. Both have served people's spiritual (and sometimes material) needs. Although different spiritualities have certainly animated them, these two traditions cannot be reduced simply to differences in

---

[96]No. 8, emphasis mine.

[97]What I have proposed in this article both clarifies and obscures, e.g., conclusions reached in documents like *The Ministry in the Church*, Roman Catholic/Lutheran Joint Commission (Geneva: Lutheran World Federation, 1982), and "Ministry and Ordination" (1973), in *The Final Report*, Anglican-Roman Catholic International Commission (Washington, D.C.: U.S. Catholic Conference, 1982) 29-39.

spirituality. Moreover, while tensions have always existed between them and have sometimes erupted into ugly and disedifying battles, the genius of Catholicism up to the present has been its ability to contain them both within itself and not settle for neat resolutions or a single church order for ministry.

3. Although there has been considerable and healthy overlap, a sort of "division of labor" has in fact prevailed between diocesan and regular clergy over the course of the centuries. The "local" or diocesan clergy has ministered primarily to the faithful according to time-honored rhythms of word and especially sacrament. Religious, when they ministered to the faithful, did so in these ways but also particularly in others that were more appropriate to special groups and circumstances: through schools or soup kitchens, through retreats or running houses for reformed prostitutes, through books and journals, or through street preaching and "revivals." This division of labor has taken the religious even further afield, away from the "faithful," in order to minister in some fashion or other to heretics, schismatics, infidels, pagans, and public sinners.

4. The division of labor is not an accident of history. It reflects the two traditions that over the course of the centuries have manifested themselves with uneven beat but with considerable consistency in ways that can only be suggested here. The vocabulary, for instance, is different. On the one hand, words like "office" and "parish" recur, while on the other we find "need" and "mission." "Hierarchy" predominates in one, whereas "fraternity" or its equivalaent is found in the other. For the one, "apostolic" indicates a conduit of authority; for the other, it suggests a style of life and ministry. For the first, ministry seems modeled on the Pastoral Epistles, the letters of Ignatius of Antioch, and the examples of Ambrose and Augustine. For the second, it seems modeled on Jesus and his disciples in the Synoptics, the itinerant Paul of his letters and Acts, and the example of the charismatic layman (later deacon) Francis. In the one instance, the model of the Church as sacrament seems especially operative; in the other, the Church as herald. The former relates more easily to "priest"—celebrant for the community and its public servant; the latter more easily to "prophet"—spokesperson and agent for special points

of view. The first generally corresponds to the "church-type," the second to the "sect-type."

5. With the bishops and the diocesan clergy the force of that first tradition is today as strong as ever, perhaps stronger. Even more than ever is it being taken as normative and in some cases, indeed, as the tradition that admits no alternative. Its central concern is still, and by the very nature of the case seems destined to remain, ministry to a *stable* community of the *faithful*. The *parish* is thus the locus of ministry par excellence.

6. It can reasonably be argued that, if such a tradition and viewpoint should utterly prevail, it would lead not to an enrichment but to an improverishment of the Church and its larger mission. "Special" ministries, which religious can by reason of tradition and interest rightly claim as peculiarly their own, seem more needed today than ever. They will, of course, take different forms than in the past in many cases, and they require more imagination and daring than seem commonly to be expended upon them. But even among the faithful, many persons seem to be falling through the cracks of "normative" ministry, at least in Western Europe and North America. Here lies the challenge for religious today.

7. Again: if such a tradition and viewpoint should utterly prevail, it would in time deprive the vast majority of religious of the center and meaning of their lives. Ministry is not something one adds to one's vocation as a Franciscan or Jesuit upon ordination to the priesthood, but something that was central and intrinsic from one's very first moment in the order, no matter how imperfectly this might be expressed by the ceremony of the vows.

8. Does not the teaching of Vatican II on the sensitive subjects with which this article has dealt need to be reviewed and enlarged? A subtle and implicit historiographical grid that seems to be widely operative in the Church today suggests that the Council has, after centuries of confusion, finally said the last word on all subjects, including these. But is this not a prideful bias towards the present that ignores the richness of the past and the potential of the future? Is it not far even from the intent of the Council itself?

9. Do we not need, therefore, especially to recover the pragmatic approach to ministry that current historiography is showing happily characterized our past, but that today seems to be ever more effectively smothered by the "normative" or by some idealized model? The abstract ideal can deliver death as well as life. In the mainline Churches—Protestant and Catholic—ennui, respectability, and dull liturgies and ministries hold sway in all too many places. It is not our "fidelity" that today needs testing, but our creativity.

10. The future of ministry in the Church is hidden in the mind of God—perhaps hidden more effectively than it has ever been. How do the laity figure into this future, how do women religious? Does religious life itself have a future? These are questions none of us can answer with any certainty. But we can try to think more adequately, and then act more appropriately, in relationship to priesthood, ministry, church order, and religious life as we actually have these institutions today.

Postscript
Tradition and Transition

The preceding studies were written over the course of a number of years and for different audiences. Under the circumstances a certain diffuseness is the almost inevitable result when they are gathered here under a single cover. I believe, however, that taken as a whole they evince an underlying unity that justifies this gathering, for they deal essentially with three basic problems related to Vatican Council II. First of all, they attempt to make a contribution towards a method for interpreting the Council. They then use the results of that contribution to discover and clarify the message of the Council—the meaning of the event and the content of the decrees. Finally, they try to suggest what the Council might signify for the present and the future of the Church. In what follows I will use this same tripartite division.

I make no claim that my treatment of any of these problems here or in the preceding pages is complete or fully satisfactory, for in dealing with them one is dealing in one way or another with the basic issue of the tradition of the Church and its meaning for our times, an issue that vastly transcends the competence of any historian or theologian. The elucidation of that issue is the ongoing task of every generation of the Christian community, but has a special urgency today because of the vast and unprecedented changes taking place in our culture that have impact on the Church. In this situation we must all do our part, however humble, according to the grace and competence that is given us.

My own training has allowed me to address the issue from a broad perspective of Christian history. While taking account of the past few decades, I have tried to reach back much further to find out where we have come from, so that we have a slightly better sense where we are—and where we might be headed. It is almost a truism to say we are in a state of transition, for such an assertion can be verified for every period of the history of Christianity. The present transition is different from others, however, in at least two respects. First, the media and our historical awareness make us more conscious of changes that are taking place. Secondly, the changes are of great proportion.

If I have little to say in these studies about the guidance of this transition by the Holy Spirit, it is not because I do not believe in that guidance but because I wish to adduce other considerations more surely within my competence. These studies are not, therefore, "studies in ecclesiology" in the usual sense of that term, but they can perhaps be regarded as studies pertinent to ecclesiology, especially to its method.

I

It is with method, therefore, that I should like to begin this retrospect. Perhaps the most basic assumption undergirding the essays in this volume is that we need to construct a method, a hermeneutic, for interpreting the Council. The documents of the Council cannot be understood without a framework of interpretation, whether we are aware of utilizing such a framework or not. This is true for all historical documents, as we concede even for the Bible, but certain features of the pronouncements of Vatican II give that assumption a peculiar relevancy for them. I have attempted to expose those features, for we are ill served by burying them, by deluding ourselves into thinking they do not exist, or by treating them with a hermeneutical naiveté that we would not tolerate for political documents and works of literature.

Historians hope to make sense of the past. In doing so they construct categories to contain and structure the mass of information, always discouragingly incomplete, that we are able to retrieve about it. With their categories they dissect and set boundaries to what was essentially a *continuum*. The debates about when ancient history ended and the Middle Ages began indicate to us that the answer to the question differs according to the data one examines and the assumptions one incorporates into the concepts "ancient" and "medieval." We cannot

escape using such historiographical constructs, for otherwise
we are destined to succumb to the view of our past that Arnold
Toynbee once stigmatized as "just one damn thing after
another."

When we employ these constructs, however, we must be
constantly aware, first of all, that they are tools of analysis that
need constant refinement and adjustment as we become aware
of the complexity of the past and of our often unexamined
assumptions regarding it. We must, secondly, realize that historians have a bias towards emphasizing a discontinuity that is
not always verified to the degree they imply to the unwary.
This is especially true when they designate certain phenomena
as reformations and revolutions. When I have used such terms
in these studies, I have perhaps too readily assumed that my
readers would be cognizant of this pitfall, so I at this point
wish emphatically to call attention to it.

It is my persuasion, nonetheless, that Catholics have an
inbred tendency to emphasize the continuities in their tradition.
Healthy though this tendency may be in many ways, it often
operates to a degree that blinds them to important discontinuities and thus beclouds their vision of both past and present. When we say that Vatican II was the twenty-first ecumenical council in the history of the Church, we are implicitly
and justifiably affirming the Council's continuity with our past.
If we are to comprehend fully the significance of the Council,
however, it is important to be aware as well of how much it
differed from similar ecclesiastical meetings. For many reasons,
some of which were utterly beyond the control of those who
organized the Council, it was unique. We do the Council and
ourselves a disservice by ignoring and failing to deal with that
uniqueness.

In other words, continuity and discontinuity are perhaps
the most fundamental historiographical categories with which
we must come to terms in interpreting Vatican II. The profound issues raised by them lie implicit in terms like reform,
renewal, reformation, and updating (*aggiornamento*) that we
use so facilely about the Council—and about similar realities
of momentous import in the history of Christianity. I must
once again here wring my hands and deplore that scholars

have shown so little interest in systematically exploring those issues.

Especially in the last essay in this volume, I have called attention to other important historiographical categories and assumptions that need our attention. We must, for instance, incorporate more effectively into our understanding of the history of our tradition what we are coming to know of the social reality affecting it. I believe that we must be especially cautious about the subtle assumption that the history of Christianity reads like a history of progress. In any case, analysis and purification of our terminology and categories of analysis must be the first step in constructing our method of interpretation.

We cannot engage in this task in a productive way, of course, unless we have an awareness of ourselves and of the impact upon us of the culture in which we live. Nobody can fully step out of that culture, true, but one of the advantages of historical studies is that they make us aware that in the depths of our consciousness lie some basic designs that in other cultures did not operate. One of the most important of these designs is what I have called "historical consciousness," but there are others. For instance, we live in a culture of multi-national corporations, at the head of each of which sits a Chief Executive Officer. When I teach Church History to my students, I have great difficulty in making them see that in the Middle Ages nobody thought of the pope as the CEO of the Church, and I shock them when I point out that that is the underlying ecclesiological design that their questions often imply—and with which they read the documents of Vatican II.

It is my contention that Vatican II was more aware of the impact that contemporary culture was having on the Church than any previous council. The Council tried as best it could to deal with both the positive and negative aspects of that reality. At a distance of some quarter of a century from the close of the Council, we are in many ways better placed to do that than were the Council Fathers themselves. As we interpret the Council, we must try to reconstruct the context in which the Council took place. It is not sufficient merely to "read the decrees." To *understand* the decrees, we must engage in the delicate and difficult task of first placing them in their historical context. Then we will understand the scope as well as the limitations of the information, assumptions, and language that the Council had at its disposal.

My final consideration concerning method has to do in fact with the language of the Council. In the foregoing essays I have called attention to it, but it needs further study as we construct our hermeneutical instrument for understanding the Council. Few aspects of the Council set it off so impressively from its predecessors and thereby suggest its uniqueness and the special care required in interpreting it. In dramatic fashion the Council abandoned for the most part the technical and principally juridical language of previous councils. What is the significance of that fact?

Viewed in the large, the style of the Council resembles the style the Fathers of the Church used in their treatises and commentaries. This similarity does not seem to be altogether accidental, for the centerpiece of the Council is without doubt *Lumen gentium*, the dogmatic constitution on the Church. Even a cursory comparison of *Lumen gentium* with Henri de Lubac's great book, *The Splendour of the Church*, reveals how dependent the former is upon the latter. In his book de Lubac proposes not only a patristic understanding of the Church but does so in a style appropriate to that understanding, as he found it in his study of the Fathers. The 1950's and 1960's saw the culmination of a revival of such studies that had its origins in the nineteenth century, so that we should not wonder that some of the *periti* at the Council would influence it in that direction.

The style is more, however, than a nostalgic recovery of a past treasure. The style is an essential part of the message. By its very discursiveness it discourages, for instance, the proof-text approach often employed in the past, for somewhere in the Council can be found a line to support almost every theological position. It thereby suggests we must enter a new realm of theological language if we are to understand what it has to say. Thus, by the very language it adopted, the Council invites us to enter into a new theological culture, a new *forma mentis*.

"The style is the man"—the style is the Council.

The theological language of the Fathers was "rhetorical" in a technical sense of the term. The Fathers were formed by the schools of rhetoric of late antiquity, where discourse was by definition persuasive—and in that way rhetorical. By their words the Fathers hoped to move their audience to a deeper appreciation of the major truths believed by all rather than to resolve questions on issues not accepted as so central to Christian faith. This quality gives their works that breadth of vision and almost perennial validity of insight for which they are so much revered. The documents of the Council echo that breadth and validity, that reluctance to close issues prematurely. This is part of the message, revealed in the style.

Vatican II is often described as a "pastoral" council. We must beware, of course, of too sharp a distinction between doctrinal and pastoral, but there is a basis for it. "Pastoral," as referred to Vatican II, means that the Council was concerned with the effectiveness in today's world of the ministry of the Church. Its style reflects that concern. The first quality of the effective rhetorician (or orator) is sensitivity to the feelings and needs of the audience.[1] The true rhetorician seeks to engage the former and to meet the latter, and thus the style is rhetorical—as is the Council's. There is thus a close affinity between rhetoric and ministry, which must also meet the feelings and needs of those to whom it is addressed.

Aggiornamento was the *leit-motif* of the Council. It meant that the Council saw that, while remaining faithful to the message of the Gospel, it must promote an articulation of theology, piety and ministry that would meet "the needs of the times." Much has been written about the ecclesiological redefinitions proposed by *Lumen gentium*, but a fundamental ecclesiological statement pervades all the documents of the Council in the very language it adopted. That statement is a

---

[1]On this issue, see John Stuart Mill, "What is Poetry?" in his *Literary Essays*, ed. Edward Alexander (Indianapolis, 1967), p. 57. See also my "Grammar and Rhetoric in the *pietas* of Erasmus," *Journal of Medieval and Renaissance Studies*, 18 (1988), 81-98, and my introduction to volume 66, *Collected Works of Erasmus* (Toronto, 1988), especially pp. xxvii-xxx.

reiteration of the basic truth that the Church is an instrument of ministry, for effective ministry by definition adapts itself to the condition of the flock. An ancient truth this, but the Council departed from the more customary emphasis on the saving power of the tradition itself to the necessity of so living and expressing it that it meet "the needs out there."

I have in my essays indicated some of the limitations of the gentle style of discourse the Council adopted and have even termed it "soft rhetoric." This means, for one thing, that the Council does not clearly tell us what it is changing, a fact that makes study of the context of its decrees all the more imperative. Without such study the decrees sound like bland truisms. They only rarely reveal a sense of before and after—we must reconstruct it. There can be no question, in any case, that we can not rightly interpret what the Council was struggling to say to us unless we take into account the medium in which it conveyed its message.

II

What was the message? The question brings me to my second point. In these studies I have several times attempted a list of some of the more important mandates that the Council specifically and explicitly issued—a more positively appreciative attitude towards other churches and religions, a new understanding of religious freedom, a recovery of episcopal collegiality, and many others. Each of these is important in itself, and any one of them would be a landmark in what is called the development of doctrine.

We must, nonetheless, be ready to rise above these extraordinarily significant particulars and turn our eyes to some even larger issues suggested by other factors peculiar to the Council, including the audience it addressed. Unlike previous councils, Vatican II intended its message in a uniquely immediate way for every member of the Church, and in *Gaudium et spes* for every man and woman of good will in the world. The media made this intention efficacious in a way earlier generations could never have imagined.

Moreover, the very bulk of the conciliar documents is a statement. That bulk dwarfs even the decrees of the Council of Trent. Implied in it is that the Council is requiring something more than acceptance of a number of decisions about certain particulars, however important they may be. It is requiring a change in mentality on the part of believers, a change in ways of looking at the Christian tradition that stretches across the board. If the Council wished to say "business as usual," it could have done so in a paragraph, and it need not have directed its documents so pointedly to such a wide audience.

Here again style and content interpenetrate. Shifts in style— shifts in "language-games"—indicate shifts in mentality and thereby even in appreciations of the way institutions of society operate. Although beforehand the Council was subjected to much speculation about what it might *define*, for instance, once in session it sedulously avoided definition. Its documents are redolent of wisdom rather than legislation.[2] Generally speaking, they invite rather than prescribe. They are religious documents.

Their repetitious use of the word "dialogue" and its equivalents helps us become aware, furthermore, of the dialogic character of their style. Collegiality itself articulates one institutional counterpart to that style and suggests the advisability of a more dialogic manner for the operations of the Church as a whole. In *Lumen gentium* the Council tries to help us understand *what* the Church is. The style of all of its documents implicitly but unmistakably teach us *how* the Church is, or ought to be. That latter teaching is of perhaps more practical relevancy for us than the former.

But the decree of the liturgy, *Sacrosanctum concilium*, perhaps best symbolizes what the Council was all about when it sought to reform the liturgy and give it a more central place in piety than it was previously believed to have held. The Council here dealt with the most delicate part of ourselves, the mode of our worship and the style of our relationship with God. The

[2]See the description of a "wisdom document" in Howard J. Gray, "What Kind of Document?" *The Way* (Supplement 61, Spring 1988), pp. 21-34.

anguish and anger evoked in some quarters by what the decree—or, perhaps more accurately, by the insensitive way it was sometimes implemented—tells us that the Council touched on what we held most dear. It touched on our religious affect and called for a conversion.

Even while professedly dealing with content, therefore, we cannot escape the question of style. The style was such to address our affect. The Council did not so much emit decisions as appeal to our good will. It tried to renew our memories of what was fundamental to us as a "community of memory," to use Robert Bellah's evocative term.[3] The Council reviewed for us the central treasures of our religious legacy and tried to inspire us thereby with hope for a more pastorally effective Church and a more humane world. This last was an important part of the conversion of mind and spirit to which it invited us.

To be more pastorally effective and to promote a more humane world, *aggiornamento* was a precondition and was the framework in which all the decrees stand. For an institution like the Church that is rightly and by definition traditional, the limitations of "adjustment to the times" are enormous, and they need not be detailed here. They directly relate to the mystery of the Incarnation as that mystery is played out in history.

I mention *aggiornamento* again only to insist that the conversion proposed by the Council dealt with understanding as well as affect. The Council said that the tradition was big and could be articulated in many traditions, consonant with the cultures of those to whom it was addressed at any given moment of time. It said that the tradition was at the same time both firm and malleable, as history had shown, and that our appreciation of it should therefore be animated more by courage than by fear. The Church was ready to act rather than to react.

The Council has subsequently been criticized for being too optimistic, and in some ways it undoubtedly was. The core of

---

[3]For a discussion of the idea, which corresponds in many ways to what Catholics mean by tradition, see Robert N. Bellah, et al., *Habits of the Heart: Individualism and Commitment in American Life* (New York, 1986), pp. 152-55.

its optimism derives, however, from discipleship to the one whose message it believed was for "all nations," for every woman and man who ever lived, no matter what their condition, their station in life or the culture in which they found themselves. The decrees of the Council thus bespeak an openness to the present and the future, and in their style they forswear premature closure on issues under debate in the Church and world.

When reviewed in the light of the above considerations, the message of the Council reveals itself as larger than the sum of the specific changes it mandated or promoted. After such a review and in the light of our experience in the twenty-five years since the Council ended, we are in a position to try to assess just how well the message has been received and what its prospects are for the future. A few words about those questions is the final task I have assigned myself in this postscript.

III

My impression is that many American Catholics would agree that the message of the Council has not been particularly well received and appropriated, but the reasons for their agreement are quite different. For the sake of discussion, we can divide these persons into two extremes, although most of us do not fit neatly into either. There are those who feel that, especially in the years immediately following the Council, the Council was badly misunderstood and was interpreted in a radical sense that distorted the tradition of the Church as well as the intentions of the Council. Their anger is sometimes almost palpable. The most extreme of this extreme repudiate the Council and, with it, the Church itself as we know it today.

On the other side are those who judge that, whatever the message of the Council, it has been muzzled in recent years and we have been set on a path of irreversible return to the former status. The Church is succumbing to a fatal failure of nerve. These persons, too, are angered. The Council tried to force new wine into old wineskins, and the skins are now spewing it forth. The extremes of this extreme also repudiate the Church by walking away from it—sometimes quietly, sometimes obstreperously.

The reasons for this situation are doubtless complex. They surely relate to the kind of education and particularly to the personality traits of the individual involved. Anger at the anger of "the others" and the almost inevitable self-justification that follows thereupon is a factor that has exacerbated the situation. As in most internecine debates, each side tends to lose sight of the validity operative in the opposing viewpoint and resorts to caricature and stigmatizing labels. It would be unrealistic to deny that these conditions have sometimes been verified relative to our understanding of both the Council and its implementation, and when they have obtained, they have obstructed judicious assessments of them.

Although these realities obfuscate our appreciation of Vatican II and of the success or failure of its implementation, they are a step removed from the Council itself. There are features endemic to the Council, it seems to me, that made some such polarization particularly likely. I must hasten to add, however, that confusion, repudiation and even bloodshed have not been unknown in the aftermath of previous councils of the Church, from earliest times up to Vatican I.

But we must concentrate on features somewhat particular to Vatican II. The first of them is what I have been discussing all along, the problem of understanding the Council and determining its full message. I believe that, for a number of reasons, some of which I have described above, the Council is not easy to interpret. That is why I believe it is so important to explicitate the method we apply to do so.

I have tried in this book to present the rudiments of what I think is required for this task—or at least the rudiments of the method I am employing. Whether critics agree or disagree with what I have presented, I hope I have at least made clear the necessity of elaborating suitable hermeneutical instruments for the Council. We cannot judge how well the message is being received unless we have some clarity about what the message is.

I have several times stated the basic elements of what I

understand that message to be, as they emerge from my method. Rather than rehearse those elements again, I can convey the point that needs to be made now by stating that I see the message to be a major challenge to long-standing ways of thinking, feeling and behaving in the Church. That challenge demands more than the acceptance of certain particulars. It demands changes in our internal frames of reference, with correlative changes in the way the Church goes about its day-by-day mission, ministry, and experience of authority.

On a sliding scale I therefore locate myself past center towards a maximal interpretation, that is, Vatican II manifests at least some of the characteristics of what I have termed a "great reformation." I cannot do other than assume that interpretation as correct as I address the question of implementation and reception.

By definition "great reformations" take a long time to work themselves into our consciousness, for they demand major shifts in perspective. They take even longer to work themselves into the institution of society. For one thing, they challenge vested interests, which do not easily surrender their "traditional" prerogatives. It took many generations for the challenge the Gregorians issued in the eleventh century to the role of lay magnates in the Church to have much practical impact.

Today a school of French historians and social scientists has called our attention to the resistance to change of all major institutions. Scholars of this so-called *Annales* school speak effectively about "la longue durée"—the persistence— of patterns of operation in these institutions, despite immense pressures from the outside to modify them. We should hardly be surprised that an institution as large and international as the Roman Catholic Church, an institution that correctly understands itself as having as its first task the obligation to hand-on unchanged the tradition it received, would be subject to this same law.

The media have conditioned us all to expect overnight miracles of transformation, but they delude us. The expectations they raise doom us to self-fulfilling disappointments. We in fact need to reexamine constantly the expectations that are often only partially explicit in our consciousness and to

challenge their assumptions. This is all the more urgent for
Vatican II because the vague purposes for which the Council
was announced raised such a variety of hopes and fears.

In all aspects of our review of Vatican II, we must try to
take as long a viewpoint as possible. At the same time, we
must not lose sight of what has happened since the Council.
The decree on religious liberty, for instance, has had immense
repercussions in many parts of the world in the way Church
and State interact and define their relationship. The various
documents related to other churches and religious has had
similar repercussions on the way Catholics behave, think and
feel relative to those institutions. Behavior that previously
might have been regarded as virtue, at least in some circles, is
now clearly seen as intolerable. In assessing the implementation
of the Council, we must avoid an exclusive focus on "not yet"
and balance it with considerations of what has already
happened.

It seems to me, however, that we must frankly admit that
what most deeply perturbs many Catholics who have an interpretation of Vatican II similar to mine is not that the Council
is misunderstood or that it is being all too slowly implemented.
What perturbs them is that they think they see that in the past
decade or so in certain quarters of the leadership in the Church
imperfectly concealed power plays are being made that obstruct even-handed discussion of the delicate issues that face
us. These plays short-circuit the dialogic style that seems to be
an important part of the message of the Council. In so far as
this judgment is verified, it indicates a level of dysfunction in
the institution destined to beget even further dysfunction.

The other side of this reality is the grievances of those who
suffered in the immediate wake of the Council from changes
that came upon them in rapid succession without adequate
explanation and with an indelicate hand. They felt that they
were asked to sacrifice overnight what they had just a few days
earlier been taught to hold most dear. Their questions were
left unanswered, their misgivings unattended, their just concerns dismissed. Power plays, however well intentioned, were
here too not unknown. Many things were done by invoking
"the spirit" of Vatican II, but such a soft expression does not

satisfy logical minds. The upheavals in society at large that marked the late sixties and early seventies added mightily to a sense of disarray and confusion.

Some reaction was therefore practically inevitable. If the message of Vatican II has the breadth and depth that I assign to it, a reaction was even more inevitable. It requires *much* of us, and we only gradually, as individuals and as an institution, assimilate such demands and realize their scope. As with similar phenomena in either secular or religious history, anybody who professes to understand them perfectly and to have appropriated them fully must be regarded with some suspicion. For their acceptance at large and their assimilation into the institutions of society, they perforce require time, a long period transition.

By reason of their great demands and wide-ranging scope, such phenomena have in history almost always been followed by attempts to recover the baby that seems to have been thrown out with the bath. They are followed, that is, by what historians designate as restorations. On the one hand, restorations balance some previous imbalances. Some of what they reinstate persists—"la longue durée."

On the other hand, they cast a pall over initiative and creative imagination, those preconditions for life-giving action. What they cannot ultimately sustain in the institution at large, however, is resistance to the general directions that culture is taking—or, if they do sustain it, they make the institution irrelevant for vast numbers of people.

As we try to understand the complex reality that Vatican II encases and to reckon with the course its implementation has taken and will take, we must again refer to the cultural context in which the Council took place and the context in which we now live. The Council explicitly wanted to put the Church in touch with that context, with "the needs of the times." Another way of stating almost the same thing is to say that the Council wanted to put the Church in touch with what I have called developments, that is, changes that have taken place in general culture that have an impact on the Church.

It is difficult to study the history of the Christian tradition without admitting that such developments have had more profound influences on the Church than most self-conscious decisions taken within the Church. Those decisions often enough reflected developments and were attempts to deal with them, which I believe in many ways hits at the heart of what Vatican II was all about. In any case, there is a symbiotic relationship between developments and such decisions. In so far as the decisions are consonant with the deepest reality of developments "out there," they make sense to most people, tend to survive in some form or other and eventually find institutional grounding.

This means that the decisions are "received" by the culture, by women and men and institutions "out there." As they are so received, moreover, they are newly translated—*quidquid recipitur secundum modum recipientis recipitur*, scholastic philosophy correctly taught us.[4] They are affected by what is out there and undergo significant changes. The decisions take on a life of their own, little under the control of their creators and only slightly more under the control of even their official interpreters. Divine providence does not seem to have exempted councils from this law. This phenomenon can be considered part and parcel of the incarnational nature of Christianity.

Those present at Vatican II only vaguely perceived the immense impact the new media of communication were having on how the Church functions. They could never have forseen the distrust of institutions of the past two decades or the rise of women's movements. Within the Church they could not have foreseen the shortage of priests, which in ways we find difficult to determine with any satisfaction reflects change in the larger culture. The encyclical *Humanae vitae* had not yet been issued, with all the as yet unresolved issues it raised in the minds of the faithful about the exercise of authority in the Church. These and many similar realities deeply affect what Vatican II means *today* and what the future course of its "implementation" will look like. In this regard the Council has a *sensus plenior*—a "fuller meaning"—that transcends original intent.

---

[4]"Whatever is received is received according to the condition of the one receiving."

The Church was assured the guidance of the Holy Spirit but never that it could prophesy or determine the precise details of the way it would move on its mysterious pilgrimage. That gift has not been granted. This means that even the Church has only a most imperfect control of its future, which is fundamentally in God's hands, not ours. We must recall these salutary truths when we reflect on "the unfinished agenda" of Vatican II.

Even in view of them, traditional Catholic teaching on the relationship between grace and human responsibility does not allow us to assume a posture of passivity regarding the Church or, in this case, regarding the meaning and implementation of Vatican Council II. God works through human agencies, respects our human dignity, makes use of our human creativity. We must therefore act each day according to the light we have.

An important part of that action, I submit, consists in looking both lovingly and critically at the Christian tradition in its broadest historical perspectives. This exercise should yield some light about the nature of our present transition. We undertake the exercise in the first instance as individuals, as I have done in these pages. But it is essentially a communitarian enterprise. As I indicated earlier, no individuals in the community that is the Church can assume that, for issues as delicate and complicated—as profoundly mysterious—as the ones we have been discussing, they have the full truth. We see, but through a glass darkly. In our darkness we see best by telling what we see straightforwardly and honestly and by listening with humility especially to those who disagree with us.

In a quite different context Robert Bellah has recommended "truthfulness about memory and about current reality, tested by critical argument and discussion in the public area."[5] That is not bad advice for us in the Church. By "memory" let us understand tradition. Let us add to the recipe prayer, humility, and the courage to act. Then we can with some serenity commit the future to God, where it properly belongs.

[5]*Individualism and Commitment in American Life: Readings on the Themes of Habits of the Heart* (New York, 1987), p. 4.

Subject Index